Dav

CANNABIS BUSINESS Startup

Easy and complete beginner's guide to legally start, run and grow your successful cannabis business. Everything you need to make money in the cannabis industry

Contents

INTRODUCTION TO CANNABIS

This book summarizes and discusses what is known about the medicinal uses of marijuana. Emphasizes evidence-based medicine (derived from knowledge and experience gained through rigorous scientific analysis) as opposed to belief-based medicine (derived from judgment, intuition, and beliefs that have not been proven by rigorous science).

Medical marijuana uses the marijuana plant or the chemicals it contains to treat a disease or condition. Medical marijuana is not used to "get high." Cannabis contains CBD, a chemical that affects the brain and improves its function without having a high value along with THC, which has analgesic properties. Both substances can be extracted and enhanced for use by short path distillation. The marijuana plant contains more than 100 different chemicals known as cannabinoids. Everyone has a different effect on the body. Delta-9-tetrahydrocannabinol (THC) and cannabidiol (CBD) are the main chemicals used in medicine. THC also creates the feeling of "high" that people feel when they smoke marijuana or eat foods that contain it.

While all states have laws requiring the use of medical marijuana, more than two-thirds of the states in the US and the District of Columbia have legalized it for medical treatments, and more bills are considering doing the same.

The cannabis industry in the United States is also growing rapidly and has created favorable business conditions in the 21st century. The cannabis industry is thriving for manufacturers, distributors and producers. Some estimates even put the cannabis industry at an annual growth rate of 16% for the next few years, so this business is expected to generate sales of 2,025, which is the current sale of a giant in the cannabis industry. These growth expectations for the sector, comparable to those of dot-com companies, have not gone unnoticed by the large investors of the first decade of this century.

Hemp is a green plant with long, blade-shaped leaves that have many small teeth on each side. It is also a strain of the Cannabis sativa species, which also includes the plant known as marijuana (Cherney 2016). However, the big difference between hemp and marijuana is that hemp does not have the same psychoactive effects as marijuana, even though it is considered part of the same species. The psychoactive compound in marijuana (THC) is only found in small amounts in hemp. This means that the compounds found in this strain have little, if any, intoxicating effects. Its stem and seeds can be used to make paper, clothing, sweeteners, packaging, and building materials.

Many currently illegal drugs such as marijuana, opium, coca, and psychedelics have been used for medicinal and spiritual purposes for thousands of years. Why are some drugs legal and others illegal today? It is not based on a scientific evaluation of the relative risks of these drugs, but it all has to do with who is associated with these drugs.

The first laws against opium in the 1870s were aimed at Chinese immigrants. The first laws against cocaine in the early 20th century were against black men in the South. In the 1970s, President Richard Nixon officially launched the war on drugs to end illicit drug use in the United States. "If we can't destroy the drug threat in America, it will certainly destroy us in time," Nixon told Congress in 1971.

Over the past four decades, the United States has devoted more than a trillion dollars to the war on drugs. Yet somehow the process has not produced the desired results: Drug use remains a very serious problem in the United States, even though the war on drugs has made these substances less accessible. The war on drugs also had several negative consequences, some of which were unintentional, including a heavy burden on the American criminal justice system and the spread of drug-related violence around the world.

In 2014, the war on drugs made a major contribution to the migrant child crisis. After some of the drug trafficking was expelled from Mexico, gangs and drug cartels intensified their activities in the northern triangle of El Salvador, Honduras and Guatemala in Central America. These countries, with their weak criminal justice and law enforcement systems, appeared unable to cope with the influx of violence and crime. The war on drugs "generated a lot of activity in Central America, a region with extremely weak systems," said Adriana Beltrán, of the Washington Bureau for Latin America. "Unfortunately, there was not a strong commitment to building the criminal justice system and the police." As a result, children fled their countries by the thousands in a major humanitarian crisis. Many of these children have ended up in the United States, where the refugee system simply cannot cope with the flood of migrant children. So is the war on drugs based on rasismo?

Through Law 1787 of 2016 and Decree 613 of 2017, the State regulated safe and informed access to cannabis and its derivatives for medical and scientific use. Said access is achieved through the Licenses granted by the competent authorities to carry out activities related to the handling of seeds for planting, cultivation of cannabis plants and transformation of cannabis for the production of psychoactive and non-psychoactive derivatives for the aforementioned purposes (doctor and scientists).

Today, marijuana is legal for recreational purposes in 11 states and Washington, DC, including Illinois and Michigan, which legalized it last year. According to Beau Kilmer, a drug policy expert at RAND, more than a quarter of the American population now lives in a state that allows marijuana for non-medical purposes. Obtaining your medical cannabis license can be preparing to apply and apply for the license

This book will teach you how to start a cannabis business: start with a good idea, discover the legwork, identify the right location, understand the legal and regulatory requirements, and much more as the book expands on them. Investing in marijuana stocks has seven aspects that are explained in the book.

Finding marijuana investors can be a very difficult task. This book describes how to attract marijuana investors to your marijuana business, grow it, and get the perfect big growth or sales you want. Opening a marijuana dispensary can also be done in any of the following ways: assess your level of commitment and eligibility, do your research, and find a rental property. There are some minor things that can ruin your cannabis business and these things are not easy to spot, they are; poorly designed logo, poor quality images, outdated website, and a lot more as mentioned in the book.

Marijuana companies often (though not always) sit on piles of cash. Whether it's a warehouse growing the plant or a retail store selling it, cannabis companies are forced to do their business with physical bills, as are many banks and credit card companies, including Visa , MasterCard and BECU, the largest credit union operating in the Washington facility, oppose it. work with them because the market is still illegal under federal law. This rejection puts everyone at risk, from employers to employees, and hinders potential economic growth.

Recreational cannabis legalization is a huge advancement in Canada and some US states that is attracting the attention of many top investors as cannabis stocks have grown exponentially, outperforming major indices and other sectors as of 2016. Legalization in the cannabis industry also offers enormous opportunities for large companies. Companies are expected to gain a significant share of the world market through mergers and acquisitions. The cannabis industry is facing significant consolidation, and the resurgence we've seen in recent years is likely just the beginning. More and more mergers and acquisitions have placed increasing importance on transparent and robust company valuations in this industry. Business automation is a smart way to simplify the tasks that can generate growth, innovation, and productivity for everyone involved. It is more than an expense, it is an investment the first step of which is to conceptualize what you want to achieve. The first investment in automation for growth is the will to do so. Then come all the technical, administrative, organizational and human aspects of implementing automation.

Since 2017, doctors in Germany can prescribe medical cannabis in the form of finished drugs, flowers and extracts. The sale of drugs containing cannabis in Germany in 2018 amounted to 83 million euros gross and the state budget itself. According to the extrapolation of the umbrella organization of pharmacists, taxes of more than 13 million euros were collected. As the demand for medical cannabis is constantly increasing, the pharmacists association expects even higher tax revenues for 2019. According to estimates, Germany had already imported cannabis drugs worth around € 52 million in June 2020. Section 280E of the Internal Revenue Code is one of the biggest complications for companies in the cannabis industry, increasing the tax burden for grow facilities, medical marijuana manufacturers and pharmacies. Finding out which expenses are deductible and which are not under IRC Section 280E can help your cannabis business make better financial decisions. The IRS considers cannabis companies that comply with state regulations to be illegal across the country and requires this to be reflected on federal tax returns. Effective Ways to Lower 280e Taxes, Cannabis Tax Types That Will Become a Multi-Site / State Cannabis Business, Mainstays of a Multi-State Cannabis Business, Multi-State Operator Challenges, Scope of Cannabis That Has Been tried. designed to create tremendous influence for executives looking for ways to circumvent the strict restrictions of digital advertising in the cannabis industry.

Corporate bankruptcy is when a business owner goes to federal court for help in settling and paying debts under the protection and guidance of a bankruptcy court. Through bankruptcy proceedings and under careful scrutiny by the federal courts, individuals and businesses can restructure their financial situation at the discretion of the bankruptcy courts without interference from creditors. And bankruptcy administration is a financial process in which a trustee (a legally appointed custodian) restructures the business to avoid bankruptcy. Once received, a court-appointed person may attempt to reverse the business or assist with the liquidation of assets and the payment of obligations, including debts, to investors.

CHAPTER 1

WHAT IS CANNABIS?

Cannabis is one of the most used drugs in the world. It is a plant that is used for recreational purposes (drugs) , medical and industrial (as raw material). There is a growing gap between the most recent marijuana science and the myth that surrounds it. Some people think that being legal in some places is safe. But your body does not distinguish a legal drug from an illegal one: it only knows the effect the drug creates once you have taken it. Cannabis use can have significant negative effects on the person who uses it.

Cannabis comes from the Indian hemp plant, the part that contains the drug is found mainly in the flowers (usually called "gems") and much less in the seeds, leaves and stems of the plant.

The hashish is light brown, dark brown or black and is dried and pressed into bars, sticks or balls. When smoked, both marijuana and hashish release a characteristic sweetish smell. Marijuana and hashish contain over 400 chemicals. The chemical that causes intoxication or the "buzz" is called THC (an abbreviation of tetrahydrocannabinol). THC creates psychotropic effects that classify marijuana as a "drug".

The dried flower petals, stems and leaves of the plant are called marijuana (grass) . Under hashish (dope shit, Piece) refers to the dried resin from the glandular hairs of the female plant. Marijuana is typically five times more effective than hashish. Acquisition, possession and trade are punishable. Dried leaves and tops of flowers of Cannabis sativa or Cannabis indica plants. Cannabis contains active chemicals called cannabinoids that cause narcotic-like effects throughout the body, including the central nervous system and the immune system. Cannabis can help treat cancer symptoms or cancer treatment side effects such as nausea and vomiting, pain, cachexia (loss of body weight and muscle mass). It is also called marijuana.

Cannabis is the name of the Indian hemp plant that contains the psychoactive ingredient tetrahydrocannabinol (THC). This active ingredient causes a state of intoxication. In our latitudes, the two types of cannabis, hashish and marijuana, are common: Plants, like animals, have characteristics that protect them in nature. Plants may have colours or shapes that hide them from predatory animals, or they may contain poisons or toxic substances that, when eaten, cause animals to fall ill or change their mental abilities, thus putting them at risk in the wilderness. THC is the protective mechanism of the cannabis plant.

You may have heard someone say that, since marijuana is a plant, it is "natural" and therefore harmless. But it is not. The hemlock, a poisonous plant, is also natural. Burning dry leaves and gems and inhaling the smoke in the lungs is certainly not "natural" and, like smoking cigarettes, can be harmful to your body.

Cannabis is a plant. People use the dried leaves, seed oil, and other parts of the cannabis plant for recreational and medicinal purposes. It can have a pleasurable effect and may soothe the symptoms of various conditions, such as chronic pain. Cannabis is also known as grass, pot, hash, weed, reefer, dope, herb, mull, buddha, ganja, joint, stick, buckets, cones, skunk, hydro, yarndi, smoke and hooch.

CHAPTER 2
HISTORY OF CANNABIS

Cannabis is a separate-sex, annual flowering plant that originates from Central Asia, more precisely from the Mongolian and South Siberian regions. There are two subspecies, Cannabis sativa and Cannabis sativa L. - commonly known as hemp. Hemp does not have any psychoactive properties like its cousin Cannabis sativa, but both were used in ancient times.

The name of cannabis comes from the Greek word κάνναβις (kánnabis), which is originally a Scythian word. The word hemp can also be a variant of a word from the same Scythian source. Later, the Scythian expressions cannabis and hemp spread throughout the Indo-European languages. In 1548, the Oxford English Dictionary documented the first use of the term cannabis sativa.

Rather, the name marijuana, or marijuana for cannabis sativa, has something of a folk etymology. The use of the word marijuana originated in Mexico among the Mexican-Spanish natives and is associated with the female name Maria Juana, but the story that connects the two is still being explored. The word was used excessively by the media in 1930 to give cannabis an alternative, alien-sounding name, to make it appear more dangerous and, in this way, to keep the American people away. Another theory is that the word marijuana comes from the Chinese word "ma" for herb. It is believed that Chinese researchers called the flower "ma ren hua", which translates as hemp seed flower.

One of the first recorded cultures to ever cultivate and use cannabis was China in 5000 BC. There is archaeological evidence of the use of hemp in ancient China. They used it to produce clothes, ropes and paper. They also used the seeds to make oil or food. The first medical use of cannabis was documented by the Chinese Emperor Shen Nung. The Chinese use cannabis effectively for pain relief and for gout.

After cannabis was spread through China, it found its way in 2000 BC. To Korea, from where around 1000 BC. Reached India. The people of India also discovered many ways to use cannabis. Like the Chinese, they used it for textiles, as a source of food and as a powerful medicine. Soon cannabis also found a way in 1400 BC. In the Middle East and was cultivated mainly by Scythians, who were Indo-Germanic nomads. It was the Scythians who brought cannabis to southern Russia and Ukraine, from which it spread to most European countries. Due to the influence of the Middle East, cannabis cultivation began to appear in Africa in the following years and at that time it also spread in parallel in most countries in Europe, Asia and Africa. The cultivation and use of cannabis were passed from one culture to another, all of whom recognized it as the most valuable harvest of their time. At the beginning of the 19th century, cannabis traveled from Africa to South America and Mexico. With so many immigrants making their way across the border in 1910-1911, it didn't take long for cannabis to reach the United States. It was there when the peaceful era of cannabis cultivation and use ended and the turbulent war on drugs began.

Unfortunately, cannabis use was linked to criminal acts committed by Hispanic immigrants, and prejudice against the herb began to rise. Many newspapers left marijuana in a bad light, and it all ended up being criminalized in the United States. The first state to ban the use of marijuana was Utah in 1915. Very many followed, and in 1931 cannabis was banned in 29 states. With the work of the "Federal Bureau of

Narcotics" and Commissioner Harry Aslinger, the "Marijuana Tax Act" was enforced throughout the United States in 1937, criminalizing all possession and use of cannabis. The law was valid for both types, whether for cannabis or hemp, regardless of the lack of psychoactive substances in the latter. Many suspected

Today's federal government still classifies marijuana as the # 1 controlled substance, stating that it has high potential for abuse and addiction without accepting medical use. While it is still illegal in many US states and European countries, the view is slowly shifting in favor of cannabis. In 1976 the Netherlands decriminalized the use of cannabis and in 1980 it was allowed to be sold in popular "coffee shops". In Spain, many private cannabis clubs have been seen calling for responsible use. The Czech Republic allowed the purchase of medical cannabis for patients with a valid prescription, although they struggle to produce it to meet medical demand.

In recent years, attitudes toward cannabis in the United States have changed, thanks to national awareness raising, 32 states have allowed marijuana for medicinal purposes. With significant amounts of new scientific research and clear evidence of the medicinal potential of cannabis, it is making its way back into the community. Hopefully the long tradition of this plant will continue to grow and flourish until it is recognized again as it was many years ago as a plant with great potential, both from a medicinal and economic point of view. It is one of the oldest crops in the world. Just over 12,000 years ago, cannabis seeds were valued as food in China. Thanks to their water resistance and elasticity, their fibers were used no later than 5000 BC and transformed into bowstrings. The analgesic effect of the plant, which results from the CBD, was also used by humans early on. Later, their quality was recognized in textile manufacturing. According to archeological findings, cannabis with a high level of THC was used for smoking at least 500 years before the beginning of our era. Celts and Germanic tribes gave their dead cannabis seeds on their way to eternity. By 500 AD, marijuana breeding had spread throughout Eurasia. The plant was sometimes so valuable that its seeds were accepted under Charles the Great as a means of payment. Hildegard von Bingen wrote to the plant whether its strong effect even healing powers. This name was only used on a total of two plants. Hemp was also invaluable in shipbuilding: Sails and ropes were extremely robust thanks to this material. Also, the ships of Christopher Columbus were loaded with the discovery of America, with about 80 tons of this material. In addition to the necessary sails and ropes, he also introduced hemp seeds. In the 19th century, medical remedies made of hemp were prescribed with particular preference, and it was not until the late 1920s that they began to be banned under the drug law. In the Americas, the more impoverished population resorted to cheap marijuana as a result of prohibition. After Harry Anslinger, commissioner of prohibition, instigated an incitement against cannabis and its consumers, panic broke out among the people. Anslinger presented marijuana as a subhuman drug that could turn people into beasts. The result was a US-wide ban on marijuana. Cannabis experienced a new boom in the 1960s-70s. It was the time of the hippies and the flower power. The time of the sexual revolution, expansion of consciousness, spirituality, and peace demonstrations. In addition to other intoxicating drugs, especially cannabis, it was consumed. While after the end of the hippie dream for a low while tide prevailed for the plant, she is experiencing a new renaissance today. Both their healing properties and their advantageous properties

18

as raw materials are being rediscovered and are introducing the plant into new areas of use. Today, about 50% of the hemp - also called hemp - are installed in automobiles. With the growing demand for organic clothing, the fabric is also in need of this area. The benefits in their function as insulating material were also recognized, and so the plant is processed into a new generation of houses. While US marijuana use is still banned at the federal level, individual member states - starting with Colorado since 2012 - have begun to do so to legalize. There are, however, different levels of regulation. So it is partly only decriminalized or allowed for medical purposes; in some cases, marijuana is also fully legalized -ab and also including private breeding. Sometimes even in the course of legalization, only cannabinoids with a low content of THC and CBD are allowed. Such prepared varieties have also been permitted in Switzerland since 2011 and are offered in so-called coffee shops. The prerequisite for this is that the THC content is less than one percent.

In the last decade, researchers have become increasingly interested in the medicinal benefits of another compound found in both plants known as cannabidiol (CBD). CBD is a non-psychoactive component of the cannabis plant but is said to help with a variety of diseases. In Europe, papermaking reached us only through Spain in the 13th century. The first paper mill in Germany was finally built-in in 1290. Until the replacement of the raw material wood for papermaking, documents and paintings were recorded on hemp. The inventor of modern book printing, Gutenberg, printed the well-known Gutenberg Bible on burlap in 1455. The US Declaration of Independence, known to us in 1776, was also recorded on hemp paper. In addition to hemp textiles in China, hemp fibers also played a significant role as a remedy in ancient Greece! Well-known scholars, such as Pliny, the Elder, reported on pain relief with hemp. Pedanios Dioscurides, a Greek physician and pioneer of pharmacology, described that the juice of hempseed would relieve earaches.

In addition to being used as a garment in ancient Greece, hemp fibers and textiles were primarily used in shipping. Tear and weatherproof sails, ropes, and ropes were manufactured here around the 17th century. In England, around 1535, Henry VIII (King of England) ordered all landowners to grow ¼ of their field with hemp. Otherwise, they were penalized. This boom of hemp cultivation lasted until the 18th century. By 1920, 80% of all textiles in the Western world were made from hemp fibers. After the decline of sailing ship traffic, the replacement by wood in the paper production, or cotton and synthetic fibers in the textile production, hemp cultivation was displaced. The reputation of the hemp plant came under pressure due to prohibition from the 1920s. It did not matter if the breeding was drug or drug hemp. Although this plant has been omnipresent for decades, centuries and millennia and is successful in our society for the treatment of many diseases such as rheumatism, tetanus, cholera, pain and inflammation, sleep disorders, migraine, Asthma, multiple sclerosis, and spasticity, even used to treat ADHD and cancer.

However, at the dawn of the modern era a crucial change has occurred in this regard. A historical reference to it is the prohibition of hemp by Napoleon in Egypt at the beginning of the 19th century. However, it is not until the beginning of the 20th century that an authentic moral and legal persecution of certain drugs is promoted. Milestones in this regard are the Shanghai Conference in 1909 and the Hague Conference in 1912 - both focused on the opium problem. In 1925 the Geneva Convention decided to include within controlled substances, along with opium, morphine and cocaine, heroin and marijuana. In 1937 the effective prohibition was consummated in North America with the sanction of the Marijuana Tax Act. At the international level, the prohibitionist policy was consolidated in 1961 with the UN Single Convention on Narcotic Drugs held in New York (it should be noted that possible medicinal uses and scientific research were excepted). This policy was endorsed by the Vienna Convention, also approved by the UN in 1971, where many synthetic substances were added to the official lists. In 1988, the Convention against Illicit Traffic in Narcotic Drugs and Psychotropic Drugs was held, where for the first time the signatories are committed to penalizing all activities related to the circulation of prohibited drugs: cultivation, manufacture, distribution, sale and money laundering.

It is relevant to note that, for more than a century, in order to substantiate their corresponding policies, certain government authorities have commissioned several scientific studies to assess the harmfulness of marijuana use. However, despite their notable coincidences regarding the denial of their supposed great danger, none of these studies had a significant influence on the implementation of the rigorous legislation. A separate mention is deserved by the Dutch government, which commissioned two studies that reached similar conclusions to the previous ones, agreeing to consider cannabis as an "acceptable risk" or "soft" drug. It was also observed that its effects depend on the context in which it is obtained and consumed. It is also pertinent to bring up the detailed Report of a Scientific Group of the same World Health Organization, entitled Use of Cannabis (Geneva, 1971). There it is pointed out that most of the studies "deny that cannabis has a pharmacological action that specifically predisposes to the use of other drugs." It is observed that one of the most frequently cited reasons for resorting to cannabis is "the feeling of well-being, relaxation and relief of tension". Conversely, paradoxically, cases have also been observed in which marijuana is used "in order to relieve fatigue and increase stamina" (as is the case of the Amazonian indigenous Tenetehara, who consume it in order to have more strength to work). Also mentioned is its common use in India "as an aid to meditation and to achieve mystical states." Although minor offenses committed by many users have been verified, no relationship was found between marijuana and violence or serious crimes. In turn, it was

23

observed that, in minority groups in the marginal sectors, aggressive behavior by cannabis users was less likely than by alcohol drinkers. Likewise, it has even been noted that "the shift from alcohol to marijuana was generally accompanied by a decrease in criminal tendencies." In minority groups from the marginal sectors, aggressive behavior by cannabis users was less likely than by alcohol drinkers. Likewise, it has even been noted that "the shift from alcohol to marijuana was generally accompanied by a decrease in criminal tendencies." In minority groups from the marginal sectors, aggressive behavior by cannabis users was less likely than by alcohol drinkers. Likewise, it has even been noted that "the shift from alcohol to marijuana was generally accompanied by a decrease in criminal tendencies."

At present there have been two significant changes in the appreciation of the qualities of this unique plant. In the first place, the medicinal property of marijuana has been rediscovered, as more and more people are turning to it to treat certain ailments - women who grow cannabis to treat problems of their children that are not alleviated by conventional drugs. Hence, for more than two decades, the number of countries that have passed laws to regulate the medicinal use of cannabis has been increasing. Within the United States, the country behind the prohibition, Oklahoma is the 30th state to do so. In Argentina last year a law was passed in this regard, however, its implementation has not yet prospered.

Second, after more than a century of prohibitionism in force, it has become clear that it has not produced the expected results - and even that it has generated more problems than solutions. In keeping with the high proportion of people breaking the law, just as medical cannabis is making its way, so is recreational cannabis. The pioneer country in legalizing it was Uruguay in 2013, and this year Canada did. Also several North American states, Colorado and Washington in principle, California later, and a month ago Vermont was the ninth. The interesting thing about these cases is that their consequences are already being studied, and so we learn that, coinciding with what was observed by the 1971 WHO report, the legalization of marijuana for recreational use in Colorado and Washington has been associated with a significant reduction in crime, especially violations and property crimes, as well as a reduction in the use of other drugs, including alcohol; at the same time, in another five states it was found that there has not been an increase in its consumption among young people, thus denying one of the main anticipatory reasons of those who still support the prohibition.

CHAPTER 3

THC AND CBD

What is THC?

The cannabinoids with a psychoactive effect are THC, cannabinol and delta-8-THC, with THC being the most powerful and abundant. Psychoactivity is the effect sought for adult or recreational use. Cannabinoids are compounds that act on the body's endocannabinoid receptors to produce various effects. Interestingly, THC binds to the same receptor in the brain as the internally produced cannabinoid anandamide , which is a chemical associated with the famous "runner's high." The amount of THC in marijuana depends both on the variety of the plant and the conditions in which it has been grown (temperature, humidity, fertilizers, substrate, etc.). In addition, initially the plant has created THCA (tetrahydrocannabinolic acid) which is in acid form and for it to become THC it has to go through a decarboxylation process.

This process is carried out at a high temperature, when we apply heat or due to the effect of radiation, that is why when marijuana is smoked or vaporized, the cannabinoids it contains are activated. It also happens if we bake the buds. There are varieties like hemp that barely contain THC and other varieties of Cannabis Sativa L. that can exceed 20%. This proportion has been increased in recent years due to the manipulation of the human being in the cultivation creating a more powerful marijuana.

THC is very poorly soluble in water so it dissolves in lipids and alcohol . The most common way of consuming it is smoking but it can also be vaped or taken with food, oils, etc. Tetrahydrocannabinol (THC) interacts with the body by connecting to receptors in the endocannabinoid system known as CB1 and CB2. THC, according to various studies, has analgesic, antiepileptic, anti-inflammatory and antiemetic properties , and its antitumor effects are also being investigated. In addition, it is used to whet the appetite and for insomnia.

What is CBD?

CBD, also known as cannabidiol, is an active ingredient (cannabinoid) that comes from the cannabis plant. It is one of the many cannabinoids found in the hemp plant. It can be used in different ways and is especially useful as a pain reliever and remedy for various diseases. In particular, CBD can relieve joint and muscle pain, as well as nervous tension. Numerous studies also show an antiepileptic and antipsychotic effect of CBD. Therefore, it is a very versatile and increasingly popular active ingredient.

"There is a lot of interest in the potential therapeutic effects of CBD, but there is very little evidence of its effectiveness," said Dr. J. Hampton Atkinson, co-director of the University's Center for Medical Cannabis Research (CMCR). of California, San Diego. CBD may have health benefits, but the lack of research in the area means that there are simply not enough data points to support most of the anecdotal claims. With that in mind, the lack of research also means that the potential health risks of CBD use are unclear.

Some research suggests that CBD can reduce anxiety and thoughts of self-criticism, and there is some evidence that CBD has antipsychotic effects in people with schizophrenia. However, other studies show no significant benefit of CBD over a placebo.

A clinical study published in the New England Journal of Medicine in 2017 found that CBD was very effective in reducing seizures in people with Dravet syndrome, a rare form of epilepsy. Then the FDA approved an oral CBD solution called Epidiolex to treat the rare disease.

There is also "great interest within the CMCR in the potential anti-inflammatory effects of CBD for use in arthritis of various types, including the knees and hands," Atkinson said. Recent in vitro research using human cell lines suffering from rheumatoid arthritis has shown that CBD treatment can help reduce inflammation. Atkinson emphasized that "CBD, like many other substances, should probably be avoided during pregnancy." Since the commercial cannabis market is largely unregulated, there is no good way to know that what you are buying is actually what you are getting in terms of dosage or product content.

In the 1980s, the system that also contains cannabinoids as a component was discovered for the first time: the endocannabinoid system (i.e. ECS). Every vertebrate has an ECS, which essentially consists of special receptors and corresponding ligands, that is, H. Substances that bind to these receptors and thus activate them. The two receptors are called CB1 and CB2 receptors. And since they are found throughout our bodies, it is believed that the ECS can affect a variety of other systems and processes in one way or another.

As a cannabinoid, CBD can interact with our endocannabinoid system. And now you can take advantage of that with a wide variety of CBD products. Simple CBD oil is still the classic, but there are now a host of alternatives to choose from based on your individual needs and preferences. CBD has received a lot of attention both in the media and academia in recent years.

Extensive research on cannabis and CBD has also given a new direction to public discourse on these topics. CBD is no longer just a part of many cannabis plants. Unlike THC, CBD draws your attention primarily for its potentially positive effects, and above all for the lack of some controversial aspects of cannabis: unlike its "bad brother" THC, CBD does not make you high, high. , plump or tense.

Now it's clear: THC is responsible for the intoxicating effects of cannabis. As we now know, THC also has many potentially beneficial effects from a medical point of view. Consequently, THC-containing flowers can also be obtained as "medical cannabis" in this context. But only with a proper prescription from the doctor. If you don't have one, THC, whatever its form, is still illegal.

CHAPTER 4

MARIJUANA SPECIES

Cannabis plants can be divided into three principal generals. These varieties originally grew in different climates and differed in appearance, growth structure, and effect.

These categories/types are:

- Indica
- sativa
- Ruderalis

Indica cannabis strains are mostly small and compact. Well suited for the so-called "homegrown," where you grow the hemp at home in a grow box. Although the plant becomes relatively small (approx.1m), indicas produce quite a lot of flowers. There are Indica cannabis strains up to 600g per m² (approx. 4-5 plants). Almost all of the indicas come from Afghanistan, Pakistan, India, Tibet, Nepal, etc., mainly from South Asia. The effect is more on the body and makes "stoned," more like a couch presser.

Indica leaves seem almost like a cartoon, and they have profoundly jagged and teardrop-shaped leaves that are made up of full and lush little fingers that are often overlaid. Each half of the smaller leaflets have a bulge that emphasizes the turgor of the plant as it leans towards the sun.

Indica plants do not grow very large and are therefore better suited for growing on a balcony or indoors. They come from the Hindu-Kush region in Central Asia. Their flowering time is relatively short: 7 to 9 weeks.

The leaves of the indica are broad and short; the plant has a "woody" structure because the branches grow much closer compared to that of Sativa.

The smell of the indica is more intense but less sweet than that of the Sativa. Indica plants have a high proportion of CBD, and their effect is, therefore, more "stoned" or relaxing. They are also better suited for medical use.

This art of the marijuana plant is justified as its sativa plant, with perception and dense budding. Since indica plants are soothing and highly damaging to the body, generally when you relax it turns to appetite, some sleepiness, or pain relief. Some have to say that you stick with it, to which the Indica strains belong.

Indica varieties have a higher amount of resin, certainly because they protect themselves from harsh climates. This resin content is perfect for managing hashish rights. This was the dominant form of consumption in the state hemisphere.

If you are new to marijuana or have heard about it for a long time, you must have heard that there are two main herbs to choose from: cannabis indica and cannabis sativa. Significant follower as to whether it is one type of cannabis or there are many, but there is a certain chemotaxonomic definition that we know belongs to the sativa and indica strains. Here we will study the morphology, the administration of cannabis indica. Change different tribes to the ones that change them. If you feel confident that you have an indica strain for yourself, choose a more robust and bushy plant than a sativa strain. Indica marijuana strains hampered high-altitude and high-altitude climates by having dense branches and short, broad-leaved leaves. It is typically 2 to 4 feet tall and has dense, wide buds rather than live blooms. These traits make them a better option for indoor growing than sativa varieties.

Those looking for real indica buds need to be careful - become the right guy with the huge new permanent weaknesses. Cannabis is one of the best known human crops, Carl Sagan suspects it is the first to be, and in recent years growers have been given unprecedented freedom to belong to hybrid varieties, to which properties to belong. Remember that each strain has access to all the others, and we are just beginning to understand how the personal chemical compounds found in cannabis, unique to marijuana, relate to the human body.

Sativa cannabis strains are mostly grown outdoors. They grow tall and wide. Therefore, Sativa strains are more for summer, when you start growing somewhere in the forest. Sativa varieties come from Thailand, Cambodia, Jamaica, Mexico, etc., mostly from tropical areas. The difference to Indicas is that the flowers take 9-12 weeks to be harvested instead of 6-9 weeks. So even longer than usual. The effect takes place more in the head and makes you "fit" rather than pushing you into the couch.

Sativa plants grow very tall, up to three meters. They grow in the areas around the equator in a relatively warm climate. The flowering period is usually relatively long: between 9 and 12 weeks. The plant itself can also continue to grow considerably during flowering. The leaves of the sativa are long and thin; the space between the branches (internodes) is more significant than that of an indicator. This gives the plant a more open appearance and is easier to harvest. The smell of Sativa is usually sweeter than that of indica. It contains a relatively large amount of THC and therefore has a slightly "high" or waking effect.

An untrimmed Sativa can become extremely large. Some plants can grow up to 5m in one season. When growing from spring to summer, these plants have long distances between branches to facilitate air circulation. In some cases, at the beginning of the flowering stage in autumn, during the differentiation, they can also double their height.

Sativas can be very different. They can have very large and densely grown inflorescences at the end of the branches, or golf ball-sized collections of flowers that are distributed all over the plant. Sativa flowers grow according to the pattern of the golden ratio, the smaller flowers almost circle the stem and forms a giant flower. The flowering phase can be very long, sometimes up to 14 weeks.

The growth in traits and appearance of Sativa is very different from that of Indica. Sativas, unlike flat-branched indexes, are similar to weeds. Fast vertical growth, large spaces between the nodes, and thinner, lighter colored leaves are Sativa traits. It's hard to confuse a lanky light green sativa with a plump dark green indica. The differences between the two species become even more apparent during flowering. Sativas will continue to gain height during their longest flowering cycle, which for true native Sativa strains can take over 16 weeks.

Without training, they can reach for the sky and stretch a lot during flowering. Outdoors, monsters over 10 feet can be collected under the right conditions. Not only are sativa leaves thin, they also have a lot more fingers than indica leaves. 9-11 fingers per leaf are common in sativas. The sativa strains were hybridized with indica to shorten flowering time and thicken bud production. It is true that pure sativa strains are low yielding and can produce loose buds that are not attractive to contemporary cannabis users. The dense indica tail is de rigueur.

The modern sativa-dominant hybrid is still growing out of most indica strains, but the buds have become much denser and are delivering more generous yields. However, the 21st century sativa bud is still not as tight as an indica pacifier. The attractiveness and yield of the pouches has been vastly improved without losing that unique sativa high. In addition, selective breeding and hybridization have significantly reduced flowering times.

Today all high quality cannabis buds have a healthy layer of icy resin. Sativa strains tend to have higher moisture tolerance, and the slightly ventilated calyx structure allows for greater resistance to mold on the buds.

RUDERALIS CANNABIS

The Cannabis Ruderalis is a subspecies of Cannabis Sativa which originates in the Himalayas and Siberia. They are short-growing plants with non-photodepent flowering periods that are shorter than that of Indica marijuana. Cannabis ruderalis is a hardy and perennial subspecies that is native to the harsh climates of Russia, Central Europe, and Central Asia. Ruderalis is believed to have originated from the well-known Cannabis indica , a subspecies that produces relatively small branches and broad leaves and is known to induce a relaxing and body-centered high among growers and users.

Ruderalis developed quite different traits compared to its botanical siblings. The ancestor of both ruderalis and indica, cannabis sativa , a tall and narrow-leaved subspecies that induces euphoric and uplifting highs, has evolved in warmer, friendlier climates. The main characteristic of these plants, as we will see later, is that they are more resistant than Indica and Sativa and they never usually grow more than 60 cm in height . The flower of the Cannabis Ruderalis plant has much less THC but more CBD than Cannabis Indica and Sativa. Therefore, it is often combined with Indica or Sativa plants to give rise to medicinal strains.

Another important difference between Ruderalis and the other subspecies of Cannabis is that it flowers automatically in 10 weeks. The light cycle does not influence the time of flowering. Therefore, Ruderalis is bred with existing strains to create an easier-to-grow autoflowering variant. The buds of the Ruderalis plant, as you may well have guessed, tend to be small but still relatively thick, and are supported by sturdy, thick stems. The stems are large because they must resist the bushy bearing of the plant. For this reason, Ruderalis marijuana allocates many resources in the reinforcement of its stems and branches.

The auto-flowering strains are a result of crossings with a ruderalis: they usually retain the favorable properties of the indica or Sativa plant, but remain relatively small and require little attention.

Autoflowering plants bloom automatically after about three weeks, regardless of the light cycle. This can be very useful for marijuana growers who want to grow cannabis outdoors in a colder climate.

The ruderal plants are not bound to the light cycles and automatically initiate the flowering phase after a predetermined growth phase. With proper handling, these plants also produce flowers that can keep up with most modern cannabis strains. However, there is one crucial difference: The flowers of the ruderalis plants are rich in CBD (with a share of up to 20%) and have only a negligible THC content. This makes them ideal for use in the cultivation of medicinal varieties. The ruderalis plants in 7-9 weeks complete the flowering phase itself.

DIFFERENCES BETWEEN SATIVA AND INDIA

A humid and warm environment characterizes the tropical climate zones. Sativa plants have adapted to these environmental conditions. They can reach 400cm in height, the internodal spaces tend to be very elongated, and the peaks are airy and soft. These characteristics allow the plants to optimize their breathing and to better withstand high humidity levels, without running the risk of being attacked by mold. The fingers of the leaves are long and thin, which allows the air to circulate inside them more quickly and efficiently. The flowering phases are over 12 weeks. The Sativa varieties are particularly suitable for open-air crops, where they can express all their properties and show their imposing size. Regardless of the cultural environment, from the coldest to the warmest and most arid climate zones, if you are going to grow them indoors, remember to provide them with enough space to develop freely. As for yields, Sativa varieties tend to produce abundant harvests simply because they become tremendous.

The Indica varieties originate from the hottest and driest deserts and mountains with the most inaccessible climates on the planet. This has led these plants to evolve by taking more compact structures to protect themselves from environmental adversities. The fingers of the leaves are squatter, the buds more compact, and the plants reach smaller heights to retain more humidity and to defend themselves from the heat of the sun and the cold of desert nights. They are particularly suitable for indoor cultivation as they maintain rather low heights, which typically oscillate between 50 and 200cm. These dimensions are perfect for smaller cultivation spaces and for crops to be kept secret. The flowering times of the Indica varieties are shorter than those of the Sativa. Plants tend to be ready for harvest after about 8-10 weeks of flowering. Although the final yields are overall lower than the Sativa, the Indica has a much higher productivity per square meter.

The classic effects of the Sativa varieties are stimulating and energizing, able to amplify concentration, mental transparency, and creativity. When you want to savor more intoxicating and active experiences, the Sativa predominant varieties are the most recommended. Among the 100% Sativa varieties, we mention the extraordinary Dr. Grinspoon and the Desfrán.

The classic effects of the Indica varieties are relaxing and "sofa-block," with sensations that can become narcotic and sedative. If you are trying to reconcile your sleep or relax on a comfortable sofa to watch a series on Netflix, then you should try the Indica varieties.

CHAPTER 5

INDOORS AND OUT DOOR MARIJUANA CULTIVATION

ADVANTAGES OF INDOOR CULTIVATION OF MARIJUANA

Certainty of harvest

The main advantage of growing indoors is the "total" control of the environment in which plants grow. Lighting, temperature, water, humidity, and CO_2 levels can be controlled relatively easily. Furthermore, it is also quite simple to keep pests and diseases under control, almost eliminating the risk of losing the crop due to atmospheric agents, mold, and parasites.

Cultivating in a closed greenhouse reduces, even in this case, almost to zero, the risk of theft and damage to the crop, and eliminates the risk of pollination, especially the accidental one.

Quick growth

Being able to control lighting and climate means managing the growth of plants to their advantage, reducing development times to less than three months instead of 7 as for outdoor cultivation.

Cyclical cultivation 12 months per year

Indoor cultivation allows us to grow Cannabis all year round free of seasonal cycles by giving us the possibility, under the guidance of our experts, to optimize our crops with a frequency ranging between 15 and 60 days depending on how you decide to set up our greenhouse.

Reduced spaces

Unlike outdoor cultivation in indoor cultivation, the spaces used are reduced to a minimum, allowing excellent quality crops already with 15/20 square meters greenhouses, storage, and drying spaces are reduced to a few square meters.

High-value collections

The cultivation of cannabis indoors is particularly indicated for the production of hemp destined for medical and food use and, therefore, subject to particular treatments, giving us profitability far superior to any other cultivable plant.

DISADVANTAGES OF INDOOR CULTIVATION OF MARIJUANA

High production costs

Start-up, management, and growth costs are higher than outdoor cultivation. Indoor cultivation requires more cultivation and maintenance than outdoor cultivation since humidity and nutrients are not present in the surrounding environment.

In any case, the expense that mostly affects a production cycle is mainly attributable to the electricity needed for the lamps, aspirators, filters, etc.

Greater commitment

Given the quality product to be obtained, it follows more considerable attention than the outdoor cultivation, and consequently, also the error margins are more restricted.

The hemp Italy consortium supports both the cultivation of light cannabis through the indoor and outdoor methodology.

The selection of mother plants takes place in different steps. In the first instance, only the plants of the female sex are selected, as the hemp genetics come from both male and female (regular) seeds.

CHAPTER 6

GENERAL OUTDOOR GROWING

STEPS TO CULTIVATING MEDICAL MARIJUANA OUTDOOR

It is necessary to know the vegetative growth of hemp, which occurs during the summer days and ends at the end of the season when the hours of light begin to gradually decrease: it is at this time that it begins to bloom. The most crucial factor for the development of the plant is precisely the light: to flower. The plant must remain exposed to light for at least 12 hours.

Normally, and especially the medicinal varieties, hemp is grown in artificial environments (the so-called indoor environments) in which the period of exposure to light is increased, which can sometimes reach up to 24 hours. The harvest, especially in the case of specimens grown for therapeutic purposes, must take place at the time of maximum flowering, in which there is a high concentration of cannabinoids. Female inflorescences and leaves are, therefore, the primary sources of active ingredients. To understand how to plant marijuana, it is necessary to know that there are two possibilities: the outdoor method and the indoor method.

The cultivation of outdoor cannabis takes place in external soils, and in this case, we deal with sowing, watering, and harvesting, all in the ground of the house, taking advantage of sunlight. It is imperative to evaluate the available spaces thoroughly: starting from the assumption that cultivation on land is by far the easiest, if you decide to grow outdoor cannabis in pots, choose a huge one. Also, place your plants in a very sunny area because, as they said, light is an essential factor for cannabis cultivation. Growing cannabis outdoors under the sun .i.e. outdoors plantation of marijuana, the following points should be noticed when choosing the location, provided you do not have your garden. Many growers prefer to grow cannabis indoors because it offers more control over the plant growth environment. However, outdoor plantations provide unique characteristics that many growers can no longer do without.

Reflection and time

Before deciding which variety to grow, you will need to find the most appropriate location for plant growth. Numerous factors can influence this decision. First of all, you will have to consider the high and low temperatures. Cannabis plants should never be grown below 12 ° C. Extreme cold can freeze or stress a plant to kill it. Similarly, temperatures above 30 ° C can cause as much damage.

Next, you will need to make sure that the plants receive enough light during the day. Depending on the regions where it is grown, the hours of sunshine can vary significantly during the different periods of the year. Find out how seasonal variations can affect cannabis crops outdoors and, if possible, talk to other growers in the area. And even if they don't have to devote themselves to cannabis cultivation, you can be sure that local farmers will understand your doubts correctly, better than anyone else.

Finally, if you have the opportunity, choose a place where your plants can be protected from the most adverse conditions, such as strong winds and rains. Place the plants indoors at night if you don't trust leaving them outside. Also, if you are growing only a couple of plants, consider using pots, which should be moved indoors if the weather worsens. Take your time to choose the right place. The right place determines the further course of the rearing and is the foundation for success or failure.

Path and accessibility

An excellent place to grow hemp should be easily accessible for the grower and, at the same time, protect from prying eyes. Since it is often necessary to take care of your hemp plants during the hemp cultivation (watering on hot days, possibly fertilizing or generally plant care, etc.), access should not be too comprehensive and expensive. However, the place should not be found by strangers or be visible for it.

Space and acreage

If you don't have your garden or land (like very few people), you have to resort to guerrilla growing (growing hemp in free natural surroundings, which you don't call your property). Make sure that the chosen location is not used for agricultural purposes, such as a farmer's field or slope. Otherwise, the hemp plants may fall victim to grazing cattle or agricultural equipment.

Soil quality

A significant point is the condition of the floor. A good soil gives the hemp plant all the vital nutrients it needs to thrive and produce a healthy and profitable hemp plant. Poor soil, in turn, can result in inhibited growth, which logically has a direct impact on harvesting, and even the death of the hemp plant. So the soil is not the same as soil, and earth is not equal to earth. It depends on the content. See also Boden Outdoor and Hanferde & Substrate.

Genetics

Once you have chosen the place to cultivate, you need to choose the seed. First of all, consider the month of harvesting of the variety you are going to grow. Then go back in time and calculate the best germination period. If you buy auto-flowering seeds, you can take advantage of the warmer summer months both for vegetative growth and for flowering, without having to worry about the light cycle (one of the many reasons why auto-flowering plants are particularly suitable for beginners).

Keep in mind that harvesting plants after October can be an invitation to molds and humidity levels that are too high. So make sure you know the difference between indica variety and Sativa variety, and how they stand out for their specific growth behavior. The predominantly indica types are best suited to the coldest and most adverse environments, while the predominantly Sativa ones prefer warmer and wetter climates. Furthermore, the Sativa varieties take a few more weeks to complete their flowering phase, further delaying the harvest date.

GERMINATION AND SOIL

The next process is to decide if you want to germinate the seeds using a particular technique or simply plant them in the ground and wait for them to sprout. By planting directly in the field, you can bypass the stress caused by the subsequent transplantation of the seedlings. If you want to use this method, put the seeds in a glass of water 24 hours before planting them. In this way, you will help them sprout and select only the best ones if the number of pots is limited.

Another way to germinate is to place the seeds between two moistened paper towels and put everything in a dark and warm place. After a few days, you will see the first shoots coming out of the seeds. At this point, plant the young seedlings in the soil. Make a small groove with a pen. If it is too deep, the plant may have difficulty developing.

Even the soil is a variable to consider very carefully before planting the seeds. If you are going to make your soil mix yourself, we have an interesting article on this topic. But if you want to buy a lot of pre-mixed earth, don't pay attention to it. You will have to do your best to make the new home comfortable for your seeds. If in your country cannabis cultivation is legal, you can ask your trusted Grow Shop for some useful advice. Otherwise, you can buy specific cannabis soil online. Do the appropriate research to avoid buying the wrong products.

Light and sun exposure

Find a place with as much sunlight as possible. Light, in this case, the sun provides the energy for photosynthesis.

Hemp is a straining plant and needs a lot of it to grow. She loves to stand in the sunlight.

So make sure that no obstacles such as trees, houses, or mountains or anything that casts a shadow directly on the cannabis plant significantly reduce the light supply.

If you have decided to add a place near such an obstacle, it would be ideal if the site was oriented to the south.

Caring for the plant

Now that the whole process is in operation, we need to make sure that the subsequent phases proceed smoothly. It is useless to try hard if you don't take care of the plants when they grow up. Irrigation will be essential, as well as knowing that there is a problem called excess water. Some growers water too often thinking of not damaging the plants, it can be hazardous. Water your plants based on soil moisture. Let the soil dry before watering the pot again. And when you spray, add water until you see it coming out of the bottom of the containers.

If you live in precipitation-rich climate zones and are growing directly in your garden, make sure you have well-drained soil. Plants grown outdoors prefer pH values between 6.0 and 7.0. It is, therefore, imperative that the waterfalls within this range. If your soil mix does not provide the correct amount of nutrients to your plants, you can make liquid fertilizers yourself. Again, too much fertilizer can damage plants or even kill them.

ADVANTAGES AND DISADVANTAGES OF THE OUTDOOR CULTIVATION

ADVANTAGES:

SIMPLICITY: It is the simplest method to grow Cannabis. Hemp per se is a powerful and infesting plant, and the Italian climate undoubtedly offers the best cradle in Europe for its growth and development.

ECONOMY : In the end, in outdoor cultivation, the only thing a seed needs to grow is a little water. No unique ventilation systems or lamps are required to start this type of farming, not to mention the total absence of costs deriving from electricity bills, given that most of the nutrients and moisture needed for proper planting are already present in the surrounding environment in a natural and almost free manner.

Outdoor grown cannabis has all the space it needs to grow, under the powerful sunlight that allows it to grow strong and healthy. It is cheap! With this, we do not want to say that in outdoor crops, no additional cost is required. Indeed, many people even spend large amounts of money to plant outdoors. However, these expenses are not entirely necessary, as is the case in indoor.

FRAGRANCE: The idea is quite widespread (although with the latest indoor tests, they are showing the exact opposite) that a flower cultivated under sunlight releases fragrances more intoxicating than one grown indoors.

DISADVANTAGES

HARVEST UNCERTAINTY: For atmospheric agents: Cannabis cultivated in the open is exposed to various environmental factors such as rain, wind, snow, storms, hail, frost, etc. These factors expose you to the risk of losing all the entire production of the year in a few hours.

For molds and pests: Cultivation in open fields (as for any other plant/vegetable) is subject to the attack of the various fungi and the multiple parasites commonly present in nature and therefore more prone to damage caused by them giving us as a result of loss of the harvest or the loss of the qualities and characteristics required by the buyers and end consumers by devaluing the selling price for the producer.

For theft and damage: Given the extreme similarity of the European hemp to the cannabis (marijuana), it often happens that raids of adolescents enter the fields to steal some plants trampling and destroying many others, even in this case affecting both the quantity and the quality of the harvest.

For pollination: In a cannabis plant, the inflorescence represents the most valuable part. Being pollinated generates seeds that subtract the quality and quantity of the crop, even devaluing the marketing value of the same. To fertilize the female plants (the only ones requested by consumers) in a field, it is also enough just a male plant within a few hundred meters.

USE OF SPECIFIC EQUIPMENT: Cultivating in the open field means large plots of land and consequently the use of costly professional equipment (Ex.: Tractors, trucks, etc.)

USE OF MANY LABOR: The cultivation of cannabis of outdoor quality requires several interventions that cannot be performed by specific machinery but exclusively by hand and plant by plant.

ONE COLLECTED PER YEAR: Since there is no control over the hours of light provided by the sun, the cultivation time follow the regular cycles of nature, offering only one harvest a year that will keep us busy from March to September (unless auto-flowering species are used which, at the expense of the quantity manufactured allow a second harvest per year).

NEED FOR LARGE COVERED VOLUMES: Let's try to imagine cultivation even of a single hectare on which thousands of plants have been sown, which must first be dried and then stored waiting for the sale. It was evident that a covered structure sufficiently large from a volumetric point of view becomes indispensable, in the final phase of cultivation, to be able to conclude and preserve in the best way the entire crop of a year.

LOW-VALUE COLLECTIONS: The cultivation of hemp in the open field is the most suitable solution for the production of plants not intended for food / medical use but for the production of hemp destined for use in green building, manufacture of paper and fabrics that therefore require low-quality plants and consequently of low cost (a few tens of euros per quintal)

REQUIRED SOIL PH FOR MARIJUANA

When growing marijuana, it is so imperative to monitor the pH levels of the growing medium and the water used to irrigate it. The correct growth of Cannabis plants depends on this parameter. As the weeks pass, the pH may change and, consequently, require a correction of its levels. Reaching the optimum pH level in the soil becomes essential. Cannabis plants tend to give the best of themselves when they grow in slightly acid soil, with a pH between 6 and 7. If you are growing hydroponically, the optimal pH is instead between 5.5 and 6.5. If your soil is too alkaline or too acidic, plant roots will have difficulty absorbing nutrients and will show stunted growth and even nutritional deficiencies. Highly acidic soil can also promote the growth of fungal diseases that can kill plants in a few days.

CHAPTER 7

MEDICAL CANNABIS

Medical cannabis refers to any part of the marijuana plant that is used to treat health problems. Medical marijuana uses the marijuana plant or chemicals in it to treat diseases or conditions. Medical marijuana is not used to get "high." Cannabis contains CBD which is a chemical that impacts the brain, making it function better without giving it a high along with THC which has pain relieving properties. Both substances can be extracted and enhanced for use through short path distillation. The marijuana plant contains more than 100 different chemicals called cannabinoids. Each one has a different effect on the body. Delta-9-tetrahydrocannabinol (THC) and cannabidiol (CBD) are the main chemicals used in medicine. THC also produces the "high" people feel when they smoke marijuana or eat foods containing it.

While every state has laws dictating the use of medical marijuana, more than two thirds of U.S. states and the District of Columbia have actually legalized it for medical treatments and more are considering bills to do the same. Yet while many people are using marijuana, the FDA has only approved it for treatment of two rare and severe forms of epilepsy, Dravet syndrome and Lennox-Gastaut syndrome.

Today, marijuana is being reevaluated on a cultural and legal level after being considered an illegal substance for decades. Recent research reports a majority of Americans support legalizing marijuana for medical or recreational use. As such, many states have legalized marijuana for either medical and recreational purposes, or both. Still, some researchers and lawmakers want to see more scientific evidence supporting specific benefits of marijuana. Aside from more research, there are concerns that marijuana's potential risks could outweigh its benefits in some cases.

BENEFITS OF CANNABIS
Chronic pain relief

There are hundreds of chemical compounds in cannabis, many of which are cannabinoids. Cannabinoids have been linked to chronic pain relief due to their chemical makeup. That is why the by-product of cannabis, such as medical cannabis, is commonly used to relieve chronic pain. This can be helpful in treating conditions that cause chronic pain, such as:

- arthritis
- fibromyalgia
- endometriosis
- migraine

Improves lung capacity.

Unlike smoking cigarettes, when you smoke cannabis in the form of cannabis, your lungs are not damaged. In fact, one study found that cannabis actually helps increase the capacity of the lungs rather than causing them any harm.

Helps to lose weight

If you look around, you will notice that the avid cannabis user is rarely overweight. This is because cannabis is linked to helping your body regulate insulin while managing caloric intake efficiently.

Regulate and prevent diabetes

With its impact on insulin, it makes sense that cannabis can help regulate and prevent diabetes. Research by the American Alliance for Medical Cannabis (AAMC) has linked cannabis to stabilizing blood sugar levels, lowering blood pressure, and improving blood circulation.

Fight cancer

One of the greatest medical benefits of cannabis is its link to fighting cancer. There is a large body of evidence showing that cannabinoids can help fight cancer or at least certain types of it.

Reduced inflammation

The CBD in marijuana is believed to help reduce inflammation. In theory, this can benefit inflammatory conditions, such as:

- Crohn's disease
- irritable bowel syndrome
- rheumatoid arthritis
- Decreasing inflammation in the body can also improve overall health.

Neurological and mental disorders

Due to its effects on the limbic system, doctors sometimes prescribe marijuana to treat the following neurological and mental health conditions:

- anxiety
- epilepsy
- multiple sclerosis
- Parkinson's disease
- post traumatic stress disorder (PTSD)
- Tourette syndrome

Helps treat depression.

Depression is quite widespread without most people even knowing they have it. The endocannabinoid compounds in cannabis can help stabilize moods, which can ease depression.

Shows promise in treating autism

Cannabis is known to calm users and control their mood. It can help children with autism who experience frequent violent mood swings to control it.

Regulate seizures

Research done on CBD has shown that it can help control seizures. Studies are underway to determine the effect cannabis has on people with epilepsy.

Repair bones

Cannabidiol has been linked to helping broken bones heal, speeding up the process. According to the Bone Research Laboratory in Tel Aviv, it also helps strengthen the bone in the healing process. This makes it harder for the bone to break in the future.

Help with ADHD / ADD

People with ADHD and ADD have trouble concentrating on the tasks at hand. They often have problems with cognitive performance and concentration. Cannabis has shown promise in promoting concentration and helping people with

ADHD / ADD. It is also considered a safer alternative to Adderall and Ritalin.

Glaucoma treatment

Glaucoma puts extra pressure on the eyeball that is painful for people with the disorder. Cannabis can help reduce the pressure applied to the eyeball, providing temporary relief for people with glaucoma.

Relieve anxiety

While cannabis is commonly known to cause anxiety, there is a way to avoid it. Taken in controlled doses and in the proper form, cannabis can help relieve anxiety and calm users.

Slow development of Alzheimer's disease

Alzheimer's disease is one of many caused by cognitive degeneration. As we age, cognitive degeneration is almost inevitable. The endocannabinoid in cannabis contains anti-inflammatories that fight inflammation in the brain that leads to Alzheimer's disease.

Coping with arthritis-related pain

Cannabis is now commonly found in the form of creams and balms that are used by people who have arthritis. Both THC and CBD help sufferers cope with pain.

Helps with PTSD symptoms

PTSD affects not just veterans, but any individual experiencing trauma. As cannabis is legalized, the impact it has on helping treat people with PTSD is being studied. Cannabis helps control the fight or flight response, preventing it from accelerating.

Helps bring relief to people with multiple sclerosis

Multiple sclerosis can be painful and cannabis is known to relieve it. Multiple sclerosis causes painful muscle contractions, and cannabis can help reduce that pain.

It reduces the side effects related to hepatitis C and increases the effectiveness of the treatment.

Treatment for hepatitis C has numerous side effects including nausea, fatigue, depression, and muscle aches. These can last for months for some people with hepatitis C. Cannabis can help reduce the side effects caused by treatment and at the same time make it more effective.

Treats inflammatory bowel diseases.

People with Crohn's disease or ulcerative colitis may find some relief with the use of cannabis. THC and cannabidiol are known to help enhance the immune response while interacting with cells that play a vital role in gut function. Cannabis helps block bacteria and other compounds that cause inflammation in the intestines.

Helps with tremors associated with Parkinson's disease.

For those who have Parkinson's disease, cannabis can help reduce tremors and pain while helping to promote sleep. It has also been shown to improve the motor skills of patients.

Help with alcoholism

Another one of the many health benefits of cannabis is that there is no question that cannabis is much safer than alcohol. While it may not be 100% risk free, it may be a smarter way to curb alcoholism by substituting it for cannabis.

DISADVANTAGES OF MARIJUANA

Risk of accident

Those who have consumed cannabis should not drive vehicles - it is also prohibited. Similar to alcohol consumption, marijuana impairs the ability to drive: The ability to concentrate is limited, and the reaction time is prolonged. Distances and speeds are misjudged. In 2016, a meta-study found that people who consumed cannabis increased the likelihood of being involved in a traffic accident by 20 to 30 percent.

Respiratory diseases

Cannabis is preferably smoked, often mixed with tobacco. This pollutes the respiratory system and the lungs. If marijuana is smoked without smoking, the balance is certainly a little better. For example, a 2005 study found only a weak correlation between pure cannabis use and lung cancer. In chronic consumption, however, the lung function decreases sharply. It also tends to cause bronchitis and chronic cough. In long-term marijuana users, bronchitis or respiratory tract inflammation is widespread.

Reduction in sexual and reproductive capacity in men

Regular users may experience decreased testosterone and libido levels. Cannabis also changes the structure of sperm, which can lead to permanent or partial sterility.

Heart attack risk

Heart disease is also one of the dangers of tobacco use. By contrast, no correlation has been found between the use of cannabis and an increased risk of myocardial infarction.

Birth Defects

Marijuana users can prematurely give birth to an above-average weightless baby. Numerous studies have also shown that cannabis use during pregnancy can cause congenital disabilities, some childhood leukemia, and psychiatric disorders from adolescence.

Mental disorders

High levels of cannabis use are likely to increase your risk of developing schizophrenia or other psychosis. There is also evidence that heavy cannabis use is associated with a slightly increased risk of bipolar disorder. Also, the risk of suicide increases with regular, energetic consumers.

Intellectual impairment

Cannabis consumption does not become stupid but affects learning ability, attention, and memory in the short term - 24 hours after use. Chronic heavy consumption limits the processing of complex information, mind, and concentration. These limitations are not healthy but are detectable through testing. However, longer-term restrictions on cognitive performance are threatened by people who have started consuming at a very young age and are consuming a lot.

CHAPTER 8

WHAT IS INDUSTRIAL HEMP?

Hemp is a crop that has grown around the world for centuries and produces food and fiber for a large number of building materials. Hemp is a green plant with long, blade-like leaves that have many small teeth on each side. It is also a strain of the Cannabis sativa species, which also includes the plant known as marijuana (Cherney 2016). However, the big difference between hemp and marijuana is that hemp does not have the same psychoactive effects as marijuana, even though it is considered part of the same species. The psychoactive compound in marijuana (THC) is only found in trace amounts in hemp. This means that the compounds found in this strain have little, if any, intoxicating effects. Its stem and seeds can be used to make paper, clothing, sweeteners, packaging, and building materials. You simply cannot "lift" a person. Marijuana looks like hemp but produces much more THC, the psychoactive chemical that led to its ban. Marijuana is nicknamed "weeds" and its long leaves are at the heart of the plant and how it is used. This is not the case with hemp. Hemp is valuable for its seed and stem. The outer part of the seed is called cake and it is fibrous and starchy. Today, cake is increasingly used as fodder. The oil is extracted from the seed, which, like many oils, has a multitude of uses, not only as fuel but also for a range of products such as varnishes, paints, and inks. Next, we will take a look at CBD oil, which is very popular right now and is one of the reasons the hemp industry is growing.

Another ingredient is walnut, which is very nutritious and rich in omega-3 fatty acids. The walnuts are now sold commercially and used in dessert products. In fact, the seed itself is sold, sometimes whole and sometimes as ground flour. Some people like to add hemp flour to muffins and cookies, homemade trails, or energy bars. The stem is the part of the plant that creates the kinds of products that many people associate with hemp. The bast fiber from the stem is made into industrial products such as clothing, bags, canvas and rope. Other elements of the stem are used to make paper and cardboard products, mainly hemp, as well as ethanol. Inside the stem is a thick, chalky substance called hurd. This dense material looks almost like drywall and is in fact used in fiberboard, concrete, and insulation, as well as animal litter and mulch.

Hemp is an industrial plant that belongs to the same family as the cannabis plants that are used to produce marijuana. It is grown on a commercial scale in many countries around the world, such as Australia, the United States, the United Kingdom, Canada, Vietnam or France. Although hemp and cannabis belong to the same plant species, they differ not only in their appearance, but also in their chemotypes (chemical compositions). Hemp, for example, has much lower levels of THC, while marijuana tends to be high in this cannabinoid. Hemp and cannabis are made for completely different reasons and often require different growing conditions. For example, cannabis, which is used to produce marijuana, has been selectively cultivated for generations to obtain female plants that produce large quantities of cannabis flowers. While hemp plants may be female, those grown for industrial purposes are generally male and do not produce flowers. These plants are also selectively grown and grown under conditions that enhance their height and the development of long, thick stems.

Industrial hemp is a very old crop that originally came from the Middle East, India, and Southeast Russia. Large, tall plants have strong stems, distinctive leaves, and no less distinctive fragrance. The scent of hemp comes from the resin that forms in female flowers. The flowers (buds) and resin have been and are traditionally used as medicines and intoxicants. The growth and flowering of the entire hemp plant, as well as the formation of the fruits and resin, blew up in just one year. The faster the growth. With its pronounced taproot, hemp has very deep roots and is at least 1.5 and sometimes up to 5 meters tall. Cannabis indica and Cannabis sativa are good in subtropics, that is, H. Adapted to hot climates. Cannabis is also a day-old plant and only blooms when the nights are long enough, that is, only in autumn! To get around this problem in temperate climates, there are crosses with cannabis ruderalis. They are known as autoflowering seeds. Another advantage of hemp ruderalis is its very low THC content with a high CBD content. Wild plants of all cannabis species, Cannabis sativa, Cannabis indica, and Cannabis ruderalis, are dioecious, which means there are female and male plants. Male plants and their flowers do not form resin. Feminized strains are preferred to increase yield, especially in tight spaces where only females bloom. Hemp fiber cultivation is widespread throughout the world with numerous varieties adapting to different climatic conditions. The varieties and origins also differ in the different contents of the more than 100 active ingredients.

WHAT IS INDUSTRIAL HEMP USED FOR?
CBD Products

One of the uses of hemp that people have recently become familiar with is in the manufacture of cannabidiol. Hemp seeds contain 20% -30% cooking oil (solid oil); 25% -30% protein, containing eight of the daily essential amino acids recommended for humans; 20% -25% fiber; 20% -30% carbohydrates; and many essential nutrients and vitamins. Unlike the marijuana plants we are more used to, hemp plants have negligible levels of THC and are rich in CBD. Since many CBD users are not interested in the psychoactive effects associated with THC, hemp is the crop of choice for farmers who make CBD products. From there, it is treated in a similar way to normal cannabis to make butter, food or oils, among other things. Hemp seed oil is used in many cosmetics and as a substitute for other industrial oils. Hemp seed oil has a pleasant taste and, like olive oil, is used as a table oil and in salad dressings. Hemp seed oil should not be used for frying or baking. When heated to temperatures above 160 ° C, the flavor diminishes and toxic by-products can form. Hemp seeds and hemp seed oil also do not have a long shelf life. Sterilization of hemp seeds (which is required when consumed in North America) can promote rancidity of the oil in the seed. If you are looking for professionally manufactured CBD products, we recommend that you do your research and find a reputable supplier. Making high-quality CBD requires a painstaking process, but the industry is unregulated, which means we have access to low-quality or even contaminated oils. Look for a manufacturer who is responsible for using CO_2 extraction and filtration and has their oils checked by third party testing.

Clothing / Fiber

Hemp was one of the first plants to be used to make fiber, and some samples of Chinese hemp fiber date back to 8000 BC. C. Fiber hemp is also used in horticultural planting materials; biodegradable mulch; pressed and molded fiber products including those used in the automotive industry; Paper and pulp products (such as hygiene products, banknotes, filters, art papers, tea bags); Building products (such as fiberboard and fiber reinforced cement board); Insulation materials; Litter for animals (made from the woody core of the plant, called hurds); Plastic biocomposites; and compressed cellulosic plastics. Hemp holds great promise as a bioenergetic culture due to its high biomass production. Hemp is still used to make clothing today and is making a comeback recently. Although hemp clothing is often associated with "hippie fashion" (such as hemp vests and baggy pants), some new designers are using this fabric to create modern items that defy this stigma.

Paper

With hemp fibers, paper can be made like wood fibers. In fact, until the mid-19th century, hemp was the main material used to make paper around the world. At this point, wood gradually began to take over. Hemp is better for papermaking than wood because it contains much more cellulose. Cellulose gives plants their structure. The more cellulose a plant contains, the more suitable it is for making paper, as fewer chemicals are required for extraction. By 1883, 90% of the world's paper was believed to be made from hemp, making it a viable alternative to wood paper.

However, due to the ban, hemp paper is not often found today. Some even believe that many corporate titans, such as chemical company DuPont and Gulf Oil, were lobbying to limit its use because of the threat hemp poses to the big business.

In general, hemp paper is stronger than wood paper and much more durable over time. Even intact hemp paper from 1500 years ago was found. Compared to wood paper, hemp paper can be recycled in many ways. Because of its natural durability, hemp paper is widely used to make roll papers in companies like RAW.

Food

Hemp seeds have received a lot of praise for their high nutritional value, as they contain high levels of protein, calcium, iron and essential fatty acids, among other things. Because of this, they are very popular as superfoods and are often sold as dietary supplements. However, hemp can also be used to make oil and milk and is often used as an additive in alcoholic beverages such as beer and wine. Plus! In fact, these seeds are so beneficial to the body that they are often classified as superfoods. Many health professionals and personal trainers believe that hemp protein supplements are much better than regular powders. There are many products for common people who just want a hemp snack or drink. For drinks, you will find refreshing hemp juices and smoothies or hemp tea if you prefer a warm and pleasant drink. But if you're looking for something sweet, crunchy hemp chocolate is delicious! It's a very tasty snack that has a mix of coffee-flavored milk chocolate, corn flakes, and a good amount of roasted hemp seeds. Once you bite into it, it becomes one of your favorite treats.

Plastic

A wide variety of plastics can be made from hemp. In fact, Ford made a prototype out of hemp and soy plastic in the 1940s. Unfortunately this vehicle was never marketed, but there is a very famous photo of Henry Ford holding an ax that proves its durability. Today, a mix of fiberglass, hemp fiber, kenaf and flax is used to make composite panels for automobiles. Hemp plastics are also used to make shower curtains, CD and DVD cases, and much more. No wonder hemp is replacing plastic. Plastic is one of the most common materials in everyday products today and is extremely harmful to the environment, especially since it is not biodegradable. Instead, hemp is 100% biodegradable. There are already alternative materials to plastic on the market, many of which are made from vegetable cellulose, an essential ingredient that is abundant in hemp. Plastic made from hemp is stronger and more environmentally friendly than plastic made from petrochemicals.

Fuel

As mentioned above, hemp can be used to make oil. And like other vegetable oils, it can be made into biodiesel. The plant can also be fermented to produce ethanol or methanol. However, the production of hemp fuel is very low as commercial biodiesel and biogas are often made from cheap materials. With fossil fuel use in decline and the use of more environmentally friendly solutions increasing, it should come as no surprise that hemp is being used as a substitute for traditional fuels. In particular, it can be used to produce biodiesel, a fuel that works in conventional diesel engines. Why hasn't this fully renewable and sustainable resource become the fashionable fuel in today's society? This could be due to the big oil companies and their attempts to suppress the hemp market, making its fuel the "only possible" option. There are many positive aspects to using hemp fuel:

> ➢ Autonomy - Hemp can be grown anywhere and is sustainable.

- It can be made at home: although it is a complex process, it is possible to make biodiesel at home.
- There would be no shortage: As a truly renewable source, there will never be a shortage of hemp.
- It's non-toxic: the process of making fossil fuels is harmful, but hemp doesn't have that problem.
- Biodegradable: Biodiesel is biodegradable and reduces the environmental impact.

Filter

Hemp can be mixed with other fibers to make all types of filters, such as: B. tea bags, coffee filters or oil filters. Hemp fibers are very tough, especially in humid conditions, which makes them an ideal material for making all kinds of filters for liquids. In fact, tea bags are often made from a combination of wood fiber and hemp, as well as plastic polymers. There are also pure hemp filters and bags that are very easy to wash and can be reused.

Construction

Hemp can be used to make a wide variety of building materials, especially insulation. Hemp could revolutionize the construction industry and make in-house production much more environmentally friendly.

Builders can use all relevant parts of hemp (oils and fibers) to restore the properties of wood, concrete, plastics, bricks, insulation materials and even coatings. "Hemp concrete" or "hemp concrete", a term that combines the words "hemp" and "concrete", is a popular formula made from hemp that can alter construction. Hemp concrete is perfect for building walls and foundations as it is seven times stronger, half as heavy and three times more flexible than conventional concrete. Hemp concrete is a valuable building material, respectful of nature and easy to work with, but currently it has a high price.

In fact, hemp is already used as an insulator in the Netherlands and Ireland, including around the world. It can also be used to make products such as particle board and pressboard, and even as a stronger, lighter and more environmentally friendly alternative to concrete known as "hemp concrete".

Beauty Products

The beauty industry already has a wide variety of creams, lotions, balms and gels made from hemp. It is known that the plant contains many extremely beneficial compounds for skin health, such as vitamins and essential acids. Hemp-based CBD creams are also used to treat some skin conditions such as eczema, arthritis, and other types of rashes, ulcers, or irritation. Hemp is full of natural nutrients, oils, and minerals that are beneficial for the skin and hair. This has often resulted in hemp being found in all types of cosmetics and skin care products. Even in countries where hemp cultivation is banned, the cosmetics industry has been able to use the beneficial phytochemicals in this plant. Hemp-derived cosmetics and skin care products include:

> Anti aging creams
> Skin cleanser
> Shaving products
> Sunscreen
> Form
> Hair care products

Water / Floor Cleaning

Hemp is sometimes referred to as "mop fruit" because it can be used to purify water or soil. For example, hemp plants are sometimes used to remove contaminants from sewage or excess phosphorus from poultry waste. This can help some farmers avoid herbicide use, which is essential for those seeking organic farming certification. One of the most interesting uses of hemp was in the 1990s when it was planted in Chernobyl, Ukraine, where it showed tremendous potential for cleaning up the land's pollution. As can be seen from the above examples, hemp is not only versatile. We don't know exactly how the hemp industry will develop, but the revival of hemp production shows a return to its widespread use in many commercial markets.

Hemp as medicine

Another very important use for hemp is in improving health outcomes. While industrial hemp is low in the cannabinoid THC, it can contain commercially viable amounts of cannabidiol (CBD). Medicines based on CBD have been shown to be beneficial in treating the symptoms of a number of debilitating conditions. Since the plant has negligible THC levels, this can alleviate concerns from authorities about allowing its cousin to be cultivated with high levels of THC. Hemp can also contain other therapeutically useful cannabinoids, but more research needs to be done to determine its medicinal potential.

Animal Food

After seeing how nutritious and beneficial hemp foods and beverages can be to humans, it is natural that this plant would also be used as animal feed. Hemp seeds are common in wild bird seed mixes as they are a good source of energy. It is well documented that birds whose diet contains hemp seeds live up to 10-20% longer, have more offspring, and can fly even longer due to improved feathers. There are hemp seed pellets for farm animals and other animals that require a much more complex diet. It is a by-product of hemp seed pressing that provides a practical and nutritious solution for animal feed. Hemp seed pellets meet the nutritional needs of most animals, whether domestic or wild. Hemp can be an effective substitute for more traditional animal feed.

CHAPTER 9

WAR ON DRUGS AND WHAT IT MEANS TODAY

Many currently illegal drugs such as marijuana, opium, coca, and psychedelics have been used for both medicinal and spiritual purposes for thousands of years. Why are some drugs legal and others illegal today? It is not based on a scientific assessment of the relative risks of these drugs - but it all has to do with who is associated with these drugs.

The US has been drug use for medical and recreational purposes since the country was founded. In the 1890s, Sears and Roebuck's popular catalog included an offer for a syringe and a small amount of cocaine for $ 1.50. (At this point, cocaine use was not yet banned). Some states passed laws banning or regulating drugs in the 19th century, and the first law of Congress to collect taxes on morphine and opium came in 1890. The 1909 Smoking Opium Exclusion Act prohibited the possession, importation, and use of opium for smoking. However, opium could still be used as a drug. This was the first federal law to ban the non-medicinal use of a substance, although many states and counties had previously banned the sale of alcohol. In 1914, Congress passed the Harrison Act, which regulated and taxed the production, import, and distribution of opiates and cocaine.

The first anti-opium laws in the 1870s were aimed at Chinese immigrants. The first anti-cocaine laws in the early 1900s were against black men in the south. The first anti-marijuana laws in the Midwest and Southwest in the 1910s and 20s were aimed at Mexican migrants and Mexican Americans. Even today, Latino, and especially black, communities are still exposed to disproportionate drug enforcement and condemnation practices. In the 1960s, when drugs became symbols of youthful rebellion, social upheaval, and political disagreement, the government stopped scientific research to assess their medical safety and effectiveness.

In the 1970s, President Richard Nixon officially launched the war on drugs to eradicate illicit drug use in the United States. "If we can't destroy the drug threat in America, it will certainly destroy us in time," Nixon told Congress in 1971. "I'm not ready to accept that alternative. Over the next few decades, especially under the Reagan administration, what." The global military and police efforts against drugs escalated. In this process, however, the drug war resulted in unintended consequences that increased violence around the world and contributed to mass incarceration in the US, even if it made drugs less accessible and reduced potential levels of substance abuse.

Nixon started the war on drugs at a time when America was hysterical about widespread drug use. Drug use had become more public and widespread by the 1960s, in part because of the counterculture movement, and many Americans believed that drug use posed a serious threat to the country and its moral standing.

Over the past four decades, the US has allocated more than $ 1 trillion to the war on drugs. In some ways, however, the process has not produced the desired results: drug use remains a very serious problem in the US, despite the fact that the drug war has made these substances less accessible. The drug war also resulted in several negative consequences, some of which were unintended, including a heavy burden on the American criminal justice system and the spread of drug-related violence worldwide. While Nixon started the modern war on drugs, America has a long history of controlling the use of certain drugs. Laws passed at the beginning of the 20th century sought to restrict the production and sale of medicines. Part of this story is racist, and perhaps the war on drugs has long hit minority communities hardest.

In response to the failures and unintended consequences, many drug policy experts and historians have called for reforms: a greater focus on rehabilitation, decriminalizing currently illegal substances, and even legalizing all drugs. The question with this policy, like the drug war in the broader sense, is whether the risks and costs are worth the benefits. Drug policy is often described as choosing between a range of bad or mediocre options rather than finding the perfect solution. In the case of the war on drugs, the question is whether the very real downsides of the ban - racially distorted arrests, drug-related violence around the world, and financial costs - are worth the potential rewards of the ban and, hopefully, the suppression of drug abuse in the US.

The aim of the war on drugs is to reduce drug use. The specific goal is to destroy and inhibit the international drug trade - to make drugs scarcer and more expensive, and thus to make drug habits in the US unaffordable. And while some of the data shows drugs are getting cheaper, drug policy experts generally believe that the drug war is still preventing some substance abuse by making the substances less accessible. The prices of most medicines, as recorded by the National Drug Control Policy Office, have fallen. Between 1981 and 2007 the median mass price for heroin fell by around 93 percent and the median mass price for cocaine powder by around 87 percent. Between 1986 and 2007, the median mass price for crack cocaine fell by around 54 percent. Meth and marijuana prices have remained largely stable since the 1980s.

Much of this can be explained by the so-called balloon effect: cracking down on drugs in one area does not necessarily reduce the overall supply of drugs. Instead, drug production and trafficking are shifting elsewhere because drug trafficking is so lucrative that someone will always want to act - especially in countries where drug trafficking is one of the few economic opportunities and governments are not strong enough to suppress it. The balloon effect has been documented in several cases, including Peru and Bolivia to Colombia in the 1990s, the Netherlands Antilles to West Africa in the early 2000s, and Colombia and Mexico to El Salvador, Honduras, and

Guatemala in the 2000s and 2010s. Sometimes the drug war has failed to curb production as a whole, as in Afghanistan. The US spent $ 7.6 billion between 2002 and 2014 to crack down on opium in Afghanistan, where much of the world's heroin supply comes from opium. Despite efforts, opium poppy cultivation in Afghanistan reached record levels in 2013. On the demand side, illegal drug use has fluctuated dramatically since the start of the drug war. The Monitoring the Future poll, which tracks illicit drug use among high school students, provides a useful clue: In 1975, four years after President Richard Nixon started the war on drugs, 30.7 percent of high school graduates reportedly used drugs the previous month. In 1992 the rate was 14.4 percent. In 2013 it was again 25.5 percent.

Still, the ban is likely to make drugs less accessible than if they were legal. A 2014 study by Jon Caulkins, a drug policy expert at Carnegie Mellon University, found that the ban multiplied the price of hard drugs like cocaine by ten times. And illegal drugs are obviously not readily available - you can't just go to a CVS and buy heroin. So the drug war is likely to stop drug use: Caulkins estimates that legalization could cause harsh drug abuse to triple, though he told me it could go much higher. But there is also evidence that the drug war is too punishable: a 2014 study by Peter Reuter of the University of Maryland and Harold Pollack of the University of Chicago found that there is no good evidence that tougher sentences or Tougher efforts to remove supplies do a better job of pressuring drug access and substance abuse than lighter penalties. So increasing the severity of the punishment doesn't do much to slow the flow of drugs.

Instead, most of the drug war's limitation on accessibility appears to be due to the simple fact that drugs are illegal, making drugs themselves more expensive and less accessible by eliminating avenues to mass production and distribution. The question is whether the potential reduction in potential drug use is worth the drawbacks experienced in other areas, including a tight criminal justice system and the global spread of violence fueled by illicit drug markets. Unless the drug war has significantly reduced drug use, production and trafficking, the cost may not be worth it and a fresh approach is preferable.

The USA uses the so-called drug scheduling system. Under the Controlled Substances Act, there are five categories of controlled substances, known as schedules, that weigh the medicinal value and potential for abuse of a drug. Medicinal value is typically assessed through scientific research, particularly large-scale clinical studies similar to those of food and drug delivery for drugs. The potential for abuse is not clearly defined in the law on controlled substances. For the federal government, however, abuse means that individuals ingest a substance on their own initiative, leading to personal health hazards or dangers to society as a whole.

According to this system, drugs on List 1 have no medical value and a high potential for abuse. List 2 drugs have a high potential for abuse, but some medicinal value. As the rank drops to Schedule 5, the abuse potential of a drug generally decreases. It can be helpful to think of the planning system as being composed of two different groups: non-medical and medical. The non-medicinal group is the list 1 drugs that are believed to have no medicinal value and high potential for abuse. The medical group consists of the drugs on lists 2 to 5, which have a certain medicinal value and are classified numerically according to their abuse potential (from high to low).

Marijuana and heroin are List 1 drugs, so the federal government says they have no medicinal value and high potential for abuse. Cocaine, meth, and opioid pain relievers are List 2 drugs, so they are considered to have some medicinal value and high potential for abuse. Steroids and testosterone products are Appendix 3, Xanax and Valium are Appendix 4, and cough supplements containing limited amounts of codeine are Appendix 5. Congress specifically excluded alcohol and tobacco from schedules in 1970. While these schedules help shape criminal penalties for illicit drug possession and sales, they are not always the last word. In 1986, for example, Congress massively increased the penalties for crack cocaine in response to concerns about a crack epidemic and its possible link to crime. And state governments can set their own criminal penalties and schedules for drugs. Other countries, such as the UK and Australia, use similar systems to the US, although their specific rankings for some drugs differ.

The US is waging the war on drugs both domestically and abroad. At home, the federal government provides local and state police forces with resources, legal flexibility, and specialized equipment to tackle illegal drugs. The local and state police then use these funds to track down drug trafficking organizations. Some of the funding, particularly from the Byrne

Justice Assistance Grant program, is encouraging local and state police to participate in drug-related operations. If the police don't use the money to track down illegal substances, they risk losing it - a financial incentive for the police to continue the war on drugs. Although the emphasis is on criminal groups, casual users are still drawn into the criminal justice system. Between 1999 and 2007, Human Rights Watch found that at least 80 percent of drug-related arrests were owned and not for sale. However, it appears that arrests for possession do not usually result in convictions and prison terms. According to federal statistics, in 2004 only 5.3 percent of drug offenders were in federal prisons and 27.9 percent of drug offenders in state prisons were in possession of drugs. The vast majority were trafficked and a few were in an unspecified "other" category.

Internationally, the US regularly supports other countries in their efforts to crack down on drugs. For example, in the 2000s, the United States provided Colombia - under what is known as Plan Colombia - with military aid and training to help the Latin American country find criminal organizations and paramilitaries funded by drug trafficking. Federal officials argue that support from countries like

Colombia is targeting the source of illicit drugs, as such substances are often made in Latin America and shipped north to the United States. But international efforts have consistently moved drug trafficking - and the violence that goes with it - to other countries, not eliminating it. In the face of the war on drugs struggling to achieve its goals, federal and state officials have begun to move away from harsh enforcement tactics and harsh criminal attitudes. The White House National Drug Control Policy Bureau is now advocating a stronger focus on rehabilitation and less on law enforcement. Even some conservatives, like former Texas Governor Rick Perry, have instituted drug courts that involve drug abusers in rehabilitation programs instead of jail or jail. The idea behind these reforms is to strike a better balance between blocking more people from drug trafficking and moving really problematic drug users to rehabilitation and treatment services that could help them. "We can't stay out of the problem," said Michael Botticelli, US drug czar, "and we really need to turn our attention to best public health strategies to make a significant difference in drug use and its consequences . " in addition in the United States. "

The escalation in the reach of the criminal justice system in recent decades, ranging from increased incarceration to the seizure of private property and militarization, can be attributed to the war on drugs. After the US escalated the drug war in the 1970s and 1980s, stricter penalties for drug offenses played a role in making the country the world's leading detention company. (But drug offenders still make up a small fraction of the prison population: approximately 54 percent of people in state prisons, where more than 86 percent of the US prison population live, were violent offenders in 2012, and 16 percent were drug offenders, according to the Bureau of Justice Statistics). Even so, mass incarceration has put a massive strain on the criminal justice system and has resulted in severe overcrowding in U.S. prisons - to the point that some states, like California, have scaled back sentences for nonviolent drug users and sellers with the express aim of reducing the incarcerated population.

In terms of police powers, the loss of civilian property was warranted to prosecute drug trafficking organizations. These losses allow law enforcement to take over the organization's assets - cash in particular - and then use the profits to fund further anti-drug operations. The idea is to turn the drug dealers' illegal profits against them. However, there have been many documented cases of police abuse of civilian property loss, including cases where the police took cars and cash from people simply because they suspected - but could not prove - that there was some type of illegal activity. In these cases, it is actually up to the people whose private property has demonstrably not done anything illegal - instead of traditional legal standards, according to which the police must prove a wrongdoing or a well-founded suspicion before acting. Similarly, the federal government helped militarize local and state police forces to better equip them to fight drugs. The Pentagon's 1033 program of providing surplus military equipment to the police force was launched in the 1990s as part of the escalation of the war on drugs by President George HW Bush. The use of SWAT teams, as reported by the ACLU, has also increased in recent decades, and 62 percent of the SWAT raids in 2011 and 2012 involved drug searches. Various groups have complained that this increase in police force is often abused and abused. For example, the ACLU argues that the loss of civilian assets jeopardizes the civil liberties and property rights of Americans, as the police can often seize assets without even bringing charges. Such seizures could also encourage police to focus on drug crimes, as a raid can result in actual money that goes back to the police, while a violent crime conviction is unlikely to do so. The Libertarian Cato Institute has also been criticizing the war on drugs for decades because drug control efforts have allowed law enforcement to expand tremendously, including wiretapping and U.S. postal research.

Police militarization became a particular sticking point during the 2014 protests in Ferguson, Missouri, over the police shooting of Michael Brown. After heavily armed police officers responded to largely peaceful demonstrators with armored vehicles that resembled tanks, tear gas, and sonic cannons, law enforcement experts and journalists criticized the tactics. Since the beginning of the war on drugs, the general trend has been to massively expand police powers and develop the criminal justice system as a means of combating drug use. But as the drug war struggles to stop drug use and trafficking, persistent measures - what many call draconian - have been challenged. If the war on drugs does not achieve its goals, critics say these additions to the criminal justice system are not worth the financial burden and cost of freedom in the United States.

The war on drugs created a black market in illicit drugs that criminal organizations around the world can rely on for revenues that fund other, more violent activities. This market generates so much revenue that drug trafficking organizations can actually compete with weak government institutions in developing countries. In Mexico, for example, drug cartels have used their profits from drug trafficking to forcibly maintain their stranglehold on the market despite the government's war on drugs. As a result, public beheadings have become a particularly important tactic of ruthless drug cartels. Up to 80,000 people died in the war. Tens of thousands of people have disappeared since 2007, including 43 students who went missing in a widespread case in 2014. But even if Mexico did actually defeat drug cartels, it may not reduce the violence in the drug war on a global scale. Instead, drug production and trafficking, and the violence associated with it, would likely shift elsewhere, since drug trafficking is so lucrative that someone will always want to step into it - especially in countries where drug trafficking may be one of the few economic opportunities and governments won't be strong enough to suppress the drug trade.

In 2014, the drug war made a major contribution to the child migrant crisis. After some of the drug trafficking was driven out of Mexico, gangs and drug cartels intensified their activities in the northern triangle of El Salvador, Honduras and Guatemala in Central America. These countries, with their weak criminal justice and law enforcement systems, appeared unable to cope with the influx of violence and crime. The war on drugs "led much activity to Central America, a region with extremely weak systems," said Adriana Beltran of the Washington Bureau for Latin America. "Unfortunately there was not a strong commitment to building the criminal justice system and the police." As a result, children fled their countries by the thousands in a major humanitarian crisis. Many of these children have ended up in the US, where the refugee system is simply unable to cope with the onslaught of migrant children. Although the child migrant crisis is quite unique in its specific circumstances and implications, the series of events - one government cracks down on drugs, human trafficking moves to another country, and drug trafficking brings violence and crime - is fairly typical in US history Drug war. In the past few decades, this has happened in Colombia, Mexico, Venezuela and Ecuador after successful drug raids in other Latin American countries. A 2012 report by the UN Office on Drugs and Crime said: "One country's success has become another's problem." This worldwide spread of violence is one of the major costs of the drug war. In assessing whether the war on drugs was a success, experts and historians weigh these costs, along with the surge in incarceration in the United States, against benefits such as potentially depressive drug use to determine whether drug control efforts have paid off.

THE WAR ON DRUGS IS BASED ON RACISM.

It is impossible to overestimate the grave racial injustices of drug control efforts around the world, which are attracting increasing attention. Last year, a group of UN experts on people of African descent found that "the war on drugs has worked more effectively as a system of racial control than as a mechanism to combat the use and trafficking of narcotics." led to mass incarceration, arbitrary arrests and detentions, and devastating police brutality, the impact of which on people of color has declined disproportionately around the world. All of this repression has sought to eradicate the illegal trade. However, year after year, United Nations data shows that the world market is growing, diversified and resilient, and the World Drug Report released today this year confirms the trend again.

In the United States, blacks are five times more likely to be incarcerated than whites, with nearly half being convicted of drug offenses. In the UK, blacks are eight times more likely to be arrested and searched than whites, while in Rio de Janeiro, Brazil, 80% of people killed by police are black. Unfortunately, little attention has been paid to the effects of these racist police policies and practices on indigenous communities. In Australia, tribal peoples are 15 to 20 times more likely to be incarcerated than non-tribal peoples. While in Canada the criminal law is repeatedly praised for following Uruguay in the legal regulation of the cannabis markets, the criminal law continues to damage black and indigenous communities disproportionately at rates similar to the US. Unfortunately, while repressive drug policies have armed the state against color communities, it's important to remember that in part they were designed for just that purpose. Traces of colonialism and racism are still anchored in the United Nations drug control system to this day. Amid the growing turmoil of anti-racist protests around the world and the collapse of monuments to colonialism and white supremacy, it is time to carefully examine the racist and culturally imperialist roots of the so-called "war on drugs" and call for corrective action. and repair. Psychoactive substances have been used by people around the world for millennia. In pre-colonial Africa and much of Asia, cannabis was grown, traded and used as medicine. The plant plays a sacred role in the Rastafarian, Sufi, and Hindu religions, and its medicinal uses are mentioned in Avicenna's Canon of Medicine, which was a medical reference text in Europe well into the 18th century. The coca leaf is revered among the indigenous peoples of the Andean-Amazon region, whose cult of the coca plant is fundamental to their culture and spirituality. While the poppy has a centuries-old history as a traditional medicine and for ceremonial use in Asia and the Middle East.

Originally, colonial interests in many parts of the world viewed these plants as important products to add to their coffers. British, French and Dutch colonial powers

103

in particular conducted lucrative trade in opium, coca and cannabis for export in their colonies in India, Burma, Indonesia, Morocco and Algeria. The British won the Opium War of 1840-42, and the victory enabled them to export opium from British India to China without restrictions. Britain defied early discussions about an opium ban as it struggled to protect its profitable opium trade.

The anti-opium movement, strongly supported by the USA, which had economic interests in weakening Europe's political and economic dominance in Asia, ultimately succeeded in laying the foundation for a global drug control system. Racism also played a key role in calling for a ban, as substances like opium and cannabis have been linked to Chinese and Mexican immigrants and African-Americans, while cocaine has been linked to black men who, according to government propaganda, seduced or turned violent American white women under their influence. After decolonization, the newly independent countries did not have the power of their colonizers to fight the strong arm of the United States to institute a global ban. The resulting international drug control regime sought to eradicate traditional practices in blatant disregard for the human rights of indigenous peoples.

The UN treaties, negotiated with the overwhelming tactics of the post-war superpowers, forced countries to criminalize and eradicate plants that had been the cornerstone of the spiritual and healing traditions of local communities for centuries. A legacy that has not been corrected to this day.

Racism and imperialism have pervaded the arguments for a ban from the start and reinforced the control of drugs as an instrument of oppression and repression. Records show that successive international drug policy conferences in the early 20th century were largely negotiated by white men who decided that psychoactive plants used by blacks and people of color should be banned while drinking brandy and smoking cigars. . Incidentally, the wine-producing countries in Europe strongly opposed efforts to create an international alcohol control agreement, revealing both the double standards of the architects of global drug control and the constant inconsistencies in the classification and control of harmful drugs. Stigmatizing certain substances and portraying them as deviant behavior has helped demonize, dehumanize, and marginalize the communities that use them. This approach justifies the application of severe penalties against certain communities that are intended to be oppressed by certain interests. John Ehrlichman, Nixon's home affairs assistant, openly admitted these tactics in 1994:

"The Nixon campaign of 1968 and the Nixon White House afterwards had two enemies: the anti-war left and the blacks. Do you understand what I'm saying? We knew we couldn't make it illegal to be against the war or to be black, but by getting the public to associate hippies with marijuana and blacks with heroin and then heavily criminalize them both, we could Disrupt communities. We could arrest their leaders, raid their homes, break up their gatherings, and slander them on the news night after night. Did we know we were lying about drugs? Of course yes. "This strategy has been used around the world to harm and suppress ethnic minorities and political differences. Recent developments in drug control have created a trend towards cannabis regulation that breaks with the prohibition regime of the last century. Uruguay, Canada and many states in the United States have established regulated markets for adult cannabis use, while several countries in Asia and Africa have begun to consider licensing medical cannabis for home use as well as production for export Attractiveness to Participate In the burgeoning global cannabis market, expected to be valued at $ 166 billion by 2025, it is now too strong to resist, and sadly these developments have left those who suffered the brunt of the war on drugs H but hardly helped. The global cannabis industry is largely owned by companies based in the global north. Traditional smallholder farmers who illegally manufactured cannabis under Prohi bition in the global south are now excluded from the legal market. In the United States, only 4% of cannabis companies are African American-owned, while Canada has refused to clear previous convictions for cannabis despite opening the adult recreational market to large companies.

A change of direction that will keep us from being prohibited is urgently needed. However, it would be deceptive if these developments continued to consolidate the postcolonial imbalances of power and privilege. The path to lifting drug bans must aim to remedy the damage that decades of bans have done to marginalized communities, and people of color in particular. Governments need to decriminalize drug use and the cultivation of banned crops, ensure full respect for indigenous rights, and separate from police and prisons. Social justice must be a central principle of legal regulation initiatives. International Day against Drug Abuse and Illicit Trafficking on June 26th is also the global day of action for the Apoye campaign. Do Not Punish, a growing community-level solidarity movement calling on governments to end punishment-based drug policies and prioritize currently underfunded health and wellness interventions. Today hundreds of local groups in more than 175 cities in 84 countries around the world will repeat the same message: it is time to end the "war on drugs" and dismantle the racist ban regime and its tools of repression. . The struggle to decolonize drug policies is critical to ending their tyranny, and it is only just beginning.

CHAPTER 10

LEGALITY OF CANNABIS

Through Law 1787 of 2016 and Decree 613 of 2017, the State regulated safe and informed access to cannabis and its derivatives for medical and scientific use. Said access is achieved through the Licenses granted by the competent authorities to carry out activities related to the management of seeds for planting, cultivation of cannabis plants and transformation of cannabis for the production of psychoactive and non-psychoactive derivatives for the aforementioned purposes (doctor and scientists).

Today, marijuana is legal for recreational purposes in 11 states and Washington, DC, including Illinois and Michigan, which legalized it last year. According to Beau Kilmer, a drug policy expert at RAND, more than a quarter of the American population now lives in a state that allows marijuana for non-medical purposes. More is likely to come: State legislatures, particularly throughout the Northeast, are openly discussing legalization, and several other states, such as Florida and Arizona, could be expanded by ballot initiative.

Most of the Democratic presidential candidates have relied on legalization. And polls have consistently found that the majority of Americans support the legalization of cannabis.

At the same time, even some advocates of legalization worry about how legalization is unfolding in the states, with concerns that a "big marijuana" industry may market marijuana irresponsibly, as companies have done. tobacco, alcohol, and opioids. And while marijuana is not as dangerous as these other legal drugs, it still presents risks, in particular, the possibility of addiction. Still, the momentum appears to be on the side of marijuana legalization, with states from New York to Florida to Arizona seen as potential candidates for legalization in the years to come.

Drug policy experts say there are alternatives to commercial legalization, such as putting state governments in charge of the production and sale of marijuana, which could dominate the for-profit incentive and give states more direct control. about the prices and who buys the marijuana. But opponents of legalization worry that any move toward legalization will inevitably attract powerful for-profit forces, especially since the marijuana industry has already taken off in several states. "The reality is that there are a myriad of other forces working here," Sabet said. Chief among them are the very powerful forces of greed and profit. When I look at how things are in states like Colorado, where the marijuana industry has a seat at the table for every state decision on marijuana policy, it worries me. " Given these concerns, opponents favor more limited reforms than legalization. Sabet, for example, said non-violent marijuana users should not be incarcerated for the drug. Other critics of legalization support the legalization of marijuana for medical purposes but not for recreational use.

Under the scheduling system, the federal government classifies marijuana as a Schedule 1 drug, meaning it is perceived to have no medical value and high potential for abuse. That classification places marijuana in the same category as heroin and a more restrictive category than Schedule 2 drugs like cocaine and methamphetamine. But that doesn't mean that the federal government considers marijuana and heroin equally dangerous drugs or that it considers marijuana to be more dangerous than methamphetamine or cocaine. The drugs in List 1 and 2 are described as having "a high potential for abuse," a vague description that does not classify the drugs in the two categories as the same or different. The big distinction between Schedule 1 and Schedule 2 substances, instead, is whether the federal government believes a drug has medical value. The DEA says that Schedule 2 substances have some medical value and Schedule 1 substances do not, so Schedule 1 drugs receive more regulatory scrutiny, even though they are not more dangerous.

There have been many calls to reschedule marijuana, but they have hit a serious hurdle: To date, there have been no large-scale clinical trials on marijuana. These types of studies are traditionally required to show that a drug has medical value to the federal government. But these studies are also much more difficult to conduct when a substance is strictly regulated by the federal government as a Schedule 1 drug. So marijuana is essentially stuck in a Catch-22 - a clinical trial may need to be rescheduled to large-scale, but those trials will be much more difficult to perform until reclassified. Congress can also pass laws to reprogram marijuana, which legalization advocates have been pushing lawmakers to do for decades. Although the scheduling system helps set up criminal penalties for the possession and sale of illicit drugs, it is not always the last word. Penalties for marijuana are generally much more relaxed than other Schedule 1 drugs, in part an acknowledgment that the drug is not as risky as, say, heroin.

Critics of legalization also argue that groceries are marketed irresponsibly, as they can take the form of kid-friendly snacks like gummy bears and cereals. So since legalization, regulators have taken a stricter approach to groceries: restricting them, requiring stronger packaging and labels, and even banning some of them. That said, it's worth noting that recreational legalization is fairly recent. The marijuana industry is still taking shape. The federal ban has made it difficult for the industry to grow big, as they cannot easily operate across state lines. How this new industry, its marketing, and its influence at all levels of government will take shape in the coming years and ultimately influence people's behavior remains very important questions for experts.

APPLICATION REQUIREMENTS FOR CANNABIS LICENCE

Completed application forms: Each of the following documents must be completed for new applications and renewal applications:

- License application
- Additional information about the license application
- Application for work licenses
- Declaration of ownership / change of directors
- Owner consent

Gather all supporting documents: In addition to the above, the following documents must be submitted:

- Certificate of compliance with tax regulations
- Land titles or documents authorizing access to or use of the property for growing marijuana
- Official police records: for the owner or all directors as well as for each employee
- Property and / or facility inspection diagram showing all different areas (with dimensions and partitions) including but not limited to entrances / exits, reception / loading areas, and storage areas.

For companies / companies / cooperatives:

Articles of association (e.g. articles of association, partnership agreement, etc.)

- Registration certificate

- Proof of application (in the case of an application under the Cooperative or Friendship Act, not yet approved)

For producer applicants:

- Consent from the potential buyer of the raw material (if available)
- Passport photo (certified by a justice of the peace)
- Copies of two (2) government-issued IDs

Submit your application by post: all completed application forms and all supporting documents should be kept in a single sealed envelope and sent to the following address:

- License and application department
- Cannabis Licensing Authority

Wait for comments from the cannabis licensing authority: The authority will review your application for completeness and notify you of any additional information that may be required. All applicants must pay a non-refundable processing fee (per license applied for). DO NOT pay this fee until the government agency asks you to provide proof of payment.

HOW DO TO GET A MEDICAL MARIJUANA LICENSE

1. Get ready to apply
2. Applies to the license

1. Get ready to apply

Know the Law: Medical marijuana laws vary greatly from state to state. Some are harder to come by than others. Knowing the law in your state will make the process easier and protect you from law enforcement.

- For example, California law allows a wide range of conditions such as cancer, anorexia, AIDS, chronic pain, spasticity, glaucoma, arthritis, migraines, or "any other disease that marijuana can provide relief". This last category is pretty broad and made it very easy to get a license in California.

- Other states, such as New Jersey, have stricter guidelines that require the existence of a "debilitating" disease and a less flexible list of eligible conditions.

- State laws also differ on how much marijuana you can own and whether you can grow your own plants.

- There are summaries of every state's law that allows the medicinal use of marijuana here. Penalties for possessing marijuana outside of medical limits also vary from state to state. You can find these fines here.
- Remember, owning any amount of marijuana regardless of the law is still a federal offense. Although federal agents generally do not care for individual patients, there is little risk of federal prosecution.
- At the federal level, the penalty for a first offense can be a fine of up to $ 1000 and / or one year in prison.
- The penalties are even more severe for giving or selling marijuana to other people. Even if it is done legally, it is considered drug trafficking.

Find out if you are eligible:

After examining the conditions under which marijuana use is allowed in your state, consider whether you are eligible.

- If you've been diagnosed with any of the conditions specifically listed in your state law, you are almost certainly entitled to a license.
- If you don't, you may still be licensed. For example, if you have symptoms that you might

consider indicative of a medical condition for which marijuana use may be permitted in your state, it is worth trying.

- However, if you have no history of symptoms or muscle injuries, you may not be able to get marijuana legally if you live in a state with strict status.
- Most states also require you to verify where you live to be eligible.

Consult a Doctor: If you think you may be eligible for a license, the next step is to find a doctor who is willing to license it. It could be your normal doctor if you have one or another.

- If you think your doctor might authorize you to use marijuana, the easiest way to go is to see them.
- If not, there are several ways to find a doctor who can give such approvals. For example, you can contact your local pharmacy as they may have contact information for a doctor in your area.
- Although your doctor cannot issue a license, it is recommended that you inform your doctor and request a reference letter and medical history documents.

Visit your doctor: make an appointment and visit your doctor for an assessment. Tell him about your condition and why marijuana could help you.

- If the doctor thinks your case is valid, they will give the necessary clearance to apply for your state license.

- In states with laxer restrictions like California, there are clinics that are dedicated to medical testing for marijuana. It doesn't take a lot of persuasion for the staff at these facilities: just tell them how marijuana can help you and they will likely approve.

- If you see a regular doctor or live in a state with stricter laws, you may need to be more persuasive. It is a good idea to come to the appointment with a good understanding of your state's law, research on how marijuana can help your condition, and information about drug safety. When you've done your homework it will be easier to do your reasoning.

- It is important that you tell your doctor that federal law does not allow you to be prosecuted for talking about or empathizing with the medical uses of marijuana

2. Applies to the license

Fill out the paperwork: Once you get your doctor's approval, most states require you to fill out a form or sign up for an approved patient registry.

- The approving doctor can dispose of the necessary documents. Otherwise, you can find it online.

- Depending on where you live, you may want to scan the doctor's records and records to send over the internet, as in the case of New Jersey. In other locations, you may need to deliver them in person, e.g. E.g. in San Diego County. Ask your doctor or inquire about requirements online.

- Paying a Fee - Most (but not all) states require payment of the license fee as well. How and where the fee is to be paid depends on the state. However, the instructions should be on your registration letterhead.

Wait for your card: Even if your stationery has been approved, don't try to buy marijuana until you have received your card. It will take most states a few days to check your papers and mail your card. In California, some clinics that run medical tests for marijuana can give you a card.

Always carry the reference document with you, stamped and signed by your original doctor: Even if you have a photo card, most pharmacies and law enforcement agencies consider the card to be invalid if it is not stamped and signed by your doctor.

Visit the pharmacy: once your card arrives, you can visit an authorized pharmacy and buy and sell marijuana.

- Most pharmacies and establishments require you to present your current ID along with your marijuana license.
- In many states like, this is the only way to get legal marijuana. Buying it elsewhere could violate state laws.

CHAPTER 11

CANNABIS: METHOD OF INTAKE

Smoked marijuana

It's the most common way of consuming marijuana. The classic joint, joint or cigarette of this plant is known to everyone. In addition to these formats, there are others through which marijuana can be consumed by inhalation, such as pipes and hookahs. In these cases, the total amount of smoke that enters the body through aspiration and the number of toxins that are created will vary. Smoked marijuana benefits the user of its ease of consumption and quick effects. We can safely say that the consumption of this plant through this system guarantees the user a maximum experience in terms of taste, smell and subsequent sensations. After several studies, it was concluded that a tremendous amount of the THC in marijuana is consumed in the combustion itself on each puff. It must also be noted that there are many varieties of seeds with different effects. Smoking is the fastest way to give birth, but it is also the most damaging to the lungs. When you decarboxylate (burn) marijuana to smoke, you get other plant and paper materials along with the cannabinoids. These foreign substances can adversely affect the delicate tissues in your lungs. If you think about it, marijuana smoking is a lot like fast food. It's quick and gets the job done, but it can get in the way of your afternoon jogging. So why smoke? If you're looking for something that differentiates smoking from the other options on this list, keep dosage size in mind.

However, marijuana users are known for their creativity and ingenuity, especially when they run out of papers. You can make bongs and pipes out of soda bottles or cans, corn on the cob, and even pieces of fruit. Marijuana smoke is carcinogenic; Therefore, the American Lung Association recommends further research to investigate the effects of marijuana use on lung health.

Vaporized marijuana
Consuming marijuana through vaporizers requires a temperature of 230 degrees, which leads to an outbreak of different types of elements with different degrees of toxicity. Inhaling through vaporizers removes the toxins created in the combustion, greatly reducing the harm to the body. It was found that at a

temperature of 180 degrees Celsius, the THC in marijuana evaporates and the hydrocarbons are no longer present. Regarding the toxicity ranking, it was concluded that the consumption of marijuana through the water pipe is more harmful than through the classic cigarette, and that this in turn is more harmful than the use of the vaporizing system.

Vaporizers (also known as vapes or vape pens) come in all shapes and sizes. The godfather of them all is the volcano that existed before marijuana was legal in a US state. The volcano's high price and size made it inaccessible to all but the most determined cannabis enthusiast. With the advances in miniaturization and the drop in prices of this technology, smaller vape pens are quickly becoming a popular alternative to joints and bongs. There are now portable and portable vapes that easily fit in your pocket. It couldn't be more convenient. Another benefit of vaporizers is that they can be used with oils that contain more than 80% THC (compared to 5-25% for flowers). As these numbers show, vaporizing oils has a much stronger effect on the body. Vaping is commonly known as the "healthiest" form of consumption because it puts far less strain on your lungs. Again, there's little science to back this up, but the smoothness of the smoke is probably the main reason cannabis users refer to it as "healthy and good for your lungs."

Infusion of marijuana

The marijuana infusion is accompanied by milk, and in it the THC in marijuana is fat-soluble instead of water-soluble (it can dissolve in fat better than water). Because of this, the infusion is done with milk and not water, which only wets the yerba without any of the desired results. It has the advantage of its tremendously easy preparation, which is not far from making a standard infusion. The milk is poured into a saucepan over low heat for ten minutes. During this time, the dried marijuana is also inside and will be removed. The moment the milk begins to rise, it is necessary to reduce the intensity of the fire. Finally, the resulting liquid must be filtered and the marijuana infusion can be taken orally.

Swallow

This method involves eating or drinking cannabis through oral tinctures, capsules, oils, or edible products. When you ingest cannabis, the active ingredients pass through your digestive system into the bloodstream to your central nervous system and your brain. Since this type of consumption takes longer to enter the bloodstream, the effect lasts longer than inhalation. This can result in more cannabis being used than intended. The effects of ingestion may also last longer than the effects of inhalation.

Marijuana sublingual

The sublingual route consists of giving any type of pill or drug orally just under the tongue. The aim is for the product or product in question to reach the body more quickly. In the case of marijuana, some pharmaceutical companies have made these types of cannabis pills that are used to provide pain relief for patients affected by diseases such as multiple sclerosis. The undeniable medicinal properties of marijuana provide the patient with muscle relaxation that leads to freedom from pain. This type of sublingual consumption requires a prior doctor's prescription so that the product can be purchased from a pharmacy.

Marijuana ointment

We are facing what is perhaps the most unusual method of using marijuana. The transdermal route (through the skin through an ointment or cream) was used in ancient times by sorcerers and shamans in indigenous areas to relieve the villagers' pain in some areas of their bodies. Today this use originated in the manufacture of a cream made by extracting the oil from marijuana with gas. This oil can be mixed with beeswax, or it can create the little-known marijuana butter, which would be another method of cannabis consumption.

CHAPTER 12

HOW TO START A CANNABIS BUSINESS

Start with a good idea:

Depending on your areas of interest and capabilities, you can choose a unique and innovative idea in the cannabis industry. There are extensive possibilities to explore through businesses that deal directly with the plant, such as the cultivation, logistics, processing and sale of cannabis. While these segments offer a wide margin for expansion and profitability, they also involve complex regulatory requirements and large capital to establish. For example, High Supplies is a 2020 cannabis industry leader dealing directly with cannabis.

Alternatively, you can explore areas like software, design, blogging, legal advice, product review, packaging and distribution relatively easy and they are quite profitable. In this case, the regulatory requirements are quite easy to meet. Make a short list of a few ideas for your business and do extensive market and field research to understand the opportunities and challenges that await you before finalizing your business idea.

Find out the footwork:

When you find an idea that you think works, it's not as simple as nailing it down and running straight to the bank with it, especially not in an industry as volatile and unpredictable as cannabis. The unfortunate truth is that even in well-intentioned states, there are many financial and even legal hurdles to overcome. But before you go through that fight, try to take a look. Find your competitors, explore their businesses, and analyze what strategies are working for them. Spend time and effort learning what it takes to delve into that particular side of the industry. Remember: starting your own headshop is a drastically different experience from starting a dispensary, which is a drastically different experience than starting a design company that specializes in outfitting grow plants, etc. There are several layers of things to consider: How much competition is there currently in that industry? What will your startup costs be like? How can you get financing? What kinds of loopholes, if any, exist?

Identify the correct location:

Location is another important factor to consider when starting a marijuana business. Businesses, such as dispensaries or product outlets, require choosing an ideal location for good foot traffic. The property must be spacious and compliant with all regulatory standards of state authorities. In case your work is primarily associated with manufacturing or cultivation, the required permits for the area, the buildings, must be in place. Perform market analysis of the user base in the existing location and competition to locate the best places to establish your business.

Second, choosing a location with favorable cannabis laws can be beneficial in easily establishing a successful business. Zoning laws can be favorable, and manufacturing permits can also be easy to acquire. The basic costs of the license, legal expenses and rent will also be optimized to support the start of your business.

Understand the legal and regulatory requirements:

The recent legalization of marijuana in several states has been a powerful step towards the commercialization of this incredible plant. But the terms of legalization, especially the regulatory standards for different cannabis businesses, vary in different jurisdictions. The absence of federal regulatory compliance indicates that you should consider local laws when deciding to start a cannabis business. Explore the regulatory policies for the cannabis business of your choice in your local area. Cannabis laws are volatile at this point, so be sure to stay up to date with the latest policies. For new business owners, taking the path of least resistance in the cannabis industry could help establish a successful business. Therefore, look for segments that have minimal regulatory requirements.

Develop a solid business plan:

A comprehensive analysis of everything you need to build a business is reflected in a solid business plan that outlines the steps, resources, and ideas required. It's not necessary 100 percent of the time, but if you're going to be looking for investor money (see up top about "acquiring funding") then it's most definitely something you're going to have to throw together. Plus, it's more important to have a solid business plan in the cannabis industry because there are just so many potential ways to slip up or accidentally forget something.

What is a business plan? Well, it's basically a single document that has the gist of everything you want your business to be. More than a detailed summary, you should also talk about your market strategy, analyze your competition, talk about finance goals and issues, and even design a rudimentary development plan (like, how will you develop your business, and how do you intend on scaling and growing it into something larger and more profitable). The business plan should provide crucial information about the company, including objectives, differentiation, areas of application, potential market opportunity, resource requirements such as financing, labor, and raw materials. You need to build a story on how these factors will help build a successful cannabis business, such as managing financial needs and operational requirements over time. A detailed business plan gives an idea of how to move forward and is also a crucial fundraising document. A cannabis business plan is quite similar to any other business, except that it is best to induce some flexibility in the plan to accommodate the evolving laws in the segment to run a successful business.

Prepare for financing:

Money is one of the most important factors in establishing your business. Sufficient funds are needed to start and run a cannabis business, from licensing costs to operating expenses. But financing could be one of the biggest hurdles for budding entrepreneurs in this industry. The reason for this is that unlike other businesses, financial institutions, such as banks, do not offer loans for new establishments in the cannabis segment. The rapid growth of the industry has attracted great interest from venture capitalists and other investors looking to explore opportunities in the area. You can take advantage of this interest to provide an impressive business plan to raise the necessary funds.

Acquire permits and licenses:

Marijuana businesses are not legalized at the federal level. Therefore, most of the licenses and registrations required for your business must be purchased from state agencies. After developing a business and financing plan, the first step is to prepare for the various legal records required to start an entity. Start by registering your business name and type of business entity, as the latter affects your tax obligations.

Next, each state has different rules for starting a cannabis business, and therefore you need to do a thorough investigation of the licenses, registrations, and permits required to open your business. The best way to ensure that you have covered all the legal requirements is to hire a legal consultant or organization to help you obtain the full list of required documents. Be sure to also complete general documentation other than specific marijuana records, such as tax records. Once you have all the formal documentation ready for your business, you are ready to start your business.

Establish the business:

Once you have all of these items in place, you are ready to begin operating your business. Be sure to speak with industry mentors to purchase advanced equipment and other necessary raw materials for your business. Keep in mind that like most other businesses, the digital marketing flow can deliver tons of benefits in reaching your customer base. Consider customer feedback to improve your business, and stay up-to-date with evolving cannabis laws that could benefit your business.

LIMITING THE RATING OF CANNABIS

Regulatory Issues: Cannabis is illegal at the federal level under the Controlled Substances Act of 1970. While the federal government is currently allowing states to self-regulate the legalization of medical or recreational marijuana, the federal government has the potential to step in and distort the industry.

Marijuana has kept many traders and investors on the sidelines due to the risk of complicity. From the expert's point of view, it is difficult to measure this risk and include it in the evaluation model.

Exceptional Tax Burdens: All profitable companies pay taxes in the United States. However, other taxable rules apply to the cannabis industry as this is illegal at the federal level and the tax authority places additional scrutiny on cannabis companies. According to IRC Section 280E, all costs, except those directly related to the manufacture, processing and storage of cannabis, must be treated as a non-deductible item when determining the taxable charge. This can result in poor profitability for successful operations. Calculating federal income tax and complying with reporting requirements can be challenging due to complex tax regulations and the lack of competent professionals to help ensure compliance with those regulations.

Constant Evolution of the Industry: The cannabis industry is constantly changing and subject to constant changes that can disrupt normal business operations. Companies in the cannabis sector invest heavily in setting up high-tech operating protocols and facilities, so any change in the industry can significantly affect those investments.

Missing market data: Applying the market approach to valuation of cannabis companies is difficult as there are no closely comparable companies and transactions to derive market multiples. Most of the companies in the cannabis industry are in the early stages reporting low or negative profits, resulting in pointless multiples. In addition, the rules and regulations in the industry differ at the state, state, and jurisdiction levels, making it difficult to compare companies that operate in different regions.

Dependency on Outlook data: Financial forecasts of the expected future cash flows in the earnings approach for valuation are made based on the effects of a variety of business scenarios over several years. Given the limited operational history of most cannabis companies, using historical data to determine expected future cash flow may not provide reliable results. In addition, the complex income tax rules that apply to the industry make forecasts even more discreet.

HOW TO INVEST IN MARIJUANA STOCKS

> ➤ Understand the types of marijuana products.
>
> ➤ Know the different types of marijuana stocks
>
> ➤ Understand the risks of investing in marijuana stocks.
>
> ➤ Know what to look for in a marijuana stock
>
> ➤ Evaluate major marijuana stocks and exchange-traded funds (ETFs)
>
> ➤ Invest with care
>
> ➤ Closely monitor changing industry dynamics

1. Understand the types of marijuana products

There are two broad categories of cannabis products:

Medical Marijuana: Medical marijuana is legally legal in 35 US states plus the District of Columbia and in more than 30 countries. Generally, a prescription from a licensed health care provider is required for patients to obtain medical marijuana; It is frequently prescribed for adults for anxiety, depression, pain, and stress.

Recreational Marijuana: Fifteen US States Plus D.C. have legalized recreational marijuana for use by adults. Recreational marijuana has been legal in Canada since October 2018 and legal in Uruguay since 2014.

2. Know the different types of marijuana stocks

There are also different types of marijuana stocks, the main three being:

Cannabis growers and retailers - These companies, which include Canopy Growth, grow cannabis (often in indoor facilities and greenhouses), harvest the crops, and distribute the end products to customers. Some also focus on operating retail stores to sell medical and / or recreational cannabis.

Cannabis-focused biotechnologies: These are biotechnology companies (such as GW Pharmaceuticals) that develop cannabinoid drugs.

Ancillary Product and Service Providers - These companies support marijuana growers by providing products and services such as hydroponics and lighting systems (a key area of focus for Scotts Miracle-Gro), packaging services, and management services.

3. Understand the risks of investing in marijuana stocks.

Investing in any type of asset carries a certain degree of risk. However, investing in marijuana stocks has specific risks that you need to understand.

Legal and Political Risks: The sale of marijuana remains illegal at the federal level in the US Additionally, US federal law places severe restrictions on banks conducting marijuana-related businesses. As a result, it is difficult for American cannabis companies to access critical financial services. Political support for legalizing or decriminalizing marijuana has grown at the federal level, but there is no guarantee that either action will take place.

Imbalances between supply and demand: Canadian marijuana growers initially undertook major expansion initiatives to increase production capacity and meet the demand for recreational marijuana. However, some companies have now reduced production. When supply exceeds demand, prices tend to drop. In this scenario, marijuana growers could see their income and profits decline, which would affect their stock prices.

Over-the-Counter (OTC) Stock Risks - OTC stocks do not have to present regular financial statements, which are important to investors as they allow them to assess the risk of stocks. They also do not have to maintain minimum market limits (the total value of the shares outstanding), which can result in a low level of liquidity (the ease with which the shares can be bought or sold without their price being affected). .

Financial constraints - Many cannabis businesses are unprofitable and face the prospect of running out of cash. They often have to raise capital by issuing new shares, which dilutes the value of existing shares. Even with this option, raising enough capital to finance growth can be challenging.

4. Know what to look for in a marijuana stock

When considering any marijuana stock to invest in, you should:

- ➢ Research the management team
- ➢ Examine the growth strategy and competitive position of the company.
- ➢ Consult company finances
- ➢ Find out how many warrants and convertible securities the company has issued (a high number could mean that the shares will be diluted in the future, which could lead to a fall in the share price)

Specific metrics to research for marijuana growers include:

- ➢ Total cost of sales per gram: includes all cannabis production costs

> ➤ Cash cost per gram: Includes all cannabis production costs except depreciation, packaging costs, and inventory adjustments.

> ➤ Marijuana growers with lower cost structures will tend to be more competitive.

5. Evaluate the main marijuana stocks and ETFs

Now for the fun part: digging into the major marijuana stocks. You can also check out exchange-traded funds (ETFs) focused on marijuana.

6. Invest carefully

What exactly does it mean to "invest carefully" in marijuana stocks? For some, particularly conservative investors, the best approach will be to avoid them altogether. Only the most aggressive investors, those who can tolerate high levels of risk, should participate. Even aggressive investors should buy only after completing the five steps above. Marijuana stocks are risky and highly volatile; It is not wise to put too much of your investment portfolio in marijuana stocks or ETFs. Consider starting with a small position in a marijuana stock. As the cannabis market grows and a company's growing income and profits confirm its investment thesis, you can add more stocks. If the growth you were counting on doesn't materialize, you need to re-evaluate your assumptions.

Also, some marijuana stocks are arguably safer than others. For example, Scotts Miracle-Gro makes most of its income outside of the cannabis industry. Historically, the company sells lawn and garden products, and that market does not face many of the risks associated with cannabis products. Less aggressive investors might prefer a stock like Scotts to a purer marijuana stock like Canopy Growth.

7. Closely monitor the changing dynamics of the industry

Generally speaking, investors are better off taking a long-term view when buying stocks. That said, the dynamics of the marijuana industry are changing rapidly. The criteria you must use to make a purchasing decision could be drastically different in a few months. Because of this, I recommend that you monitor the stocks of marijuana or ETFs you buy, along with the industry in general, very closely and frequently. Some changes could be beneficial, for example a possible relaxation of US federal marijuana laws. However, other changes could be bad news, such as the possibility that European medical cannabis markets may not grow as fast as they are. I expected.

HOW TO FIND CANNABIS INVESTORS
Using cannabis business directories

Business directories are long lists of businesses that often cater to specific industries and interests. Cannabis business directories are a fantastic place for companies to list themselves to gain traction, improve SEO, and make themselves visible to prospects and clients. They can also be an excellent source for finding cannabis investors. Many investors use these directories to find interesting cannabis startups and businesses in need of financing. Listing yourself in as many directories as possible can be a good way to start generating interest. Business directories can be especially helpful for startups, both for finding investors and for gaining some traction. You can also communicate with investors through cannabis company directories. Some directories, like Cannapany, cater to investors, making them ideal for listing your startup. But many others, like Ganjapreneur and The Cannabis Business Directory, can also help you attract the attention of potential investors.

Attend cannabis industry events

Another great way to find cannabis investors is to attend cannabis industry events and expeditions. These events are great for many reasons: they often include speeches and seminars to help cannabis companies, give companies a chance to get their name out there, and put on the perfect event. way to interact with industry professionals face-to-face.

Networking at cannabis events often gives you the opportunity to meet new clients, especially if you are a B2B cannabis business service. They are also ideal for meeting investors. If you meet interested investors in person, you have the opportunity to introduce yourself directly and get them interested in what you have to offer. Some of these events are even designed for investors, such as the Cannabis Investor Forum, but you can find enthusiastic cannabis investors at all kinds of industry events. Make sure to prepare ahead of time. Having a solid pitch and being able to showcase the potential success of your business can go a long way when it comes to getting investors interested.

Online network

Although face-to-face meetings are often important to investors, online networking is an incredibly effective way to meet potential investors in today's digital age. Many companies find potential investors through social media, forums, and dedicated industry websites. Using online networks can be a very effective way to meet potential investors. There are many ways of doing it. You may want to join cannabis-related groups on social media platforms like LinkedIn. There are many LinkedIn cannabis groups for networking where you can often find investors. You can also use cannabis social media. While some of these are designed solely for social use, there are business-focused cannabis social networks like WeedCircles. Knowing how to reach investors with a solid business plan and proposal will help here. While it's helpful to meet or call investors to discuss the details of your business, websites and social media are great places to find and connect with investors in the first place.

Ask your colleagues

One of the easiest ways to find investors for your cannabis business is to simply ask. Many businesses start when friends ask colleagues for help with financing. You can end up with an interest-free investment or even a new business partner. It is best to start by asking your professional contacts. This is especially helpful if you know people in the industry.

Asking to see if someone wants to invest in your startup or if they know someone who might be interested could lead to the perfect opportunity. You can also ask family and friends. In fact, many entrepreneurs raise funds for their businesses by asking family and friends to invest. Although it is still important to pay them back, it is generally much easier than other ways of financing. Regardless of who you ask to help you with financing, be sure to present your business plan and let them know what to expect in terms of profit.

Use crowdfunding

In recent years, crowdfunding has become an extremely popular way for startups to raise funds, as well as allowing interested consumers to act as investors. There are many online crowdfunding platforms where you can present your business idea and request financing. Some companies start out with investments from crowdfunding companies without paying anything back. However, it is best to offer your sponsors some type of incentive or compensation as a common courtesy, as well as to capture their interest.

THE BEST INVESTMENTS FOR INCOME

1. High Yield Savings Accounts
2. Certificates of Deposit (CD)
3. Money market funds
4. Government bonds
5. Corporate bonds
6. Mutual funds
7. Index funds
8. Exchange-traded funds (ETFs)
9. Dividend shares
10. Individual actions
11. Alternative investments
12. Real estate

1. High Yield Savings Accounts

Online savings accounts and cash management accounts provide higher rates of return than what you will get from a traditional checking or savings bank account. Cash management accounts are like a hybrid between savings and checking accounts: they can pay similar interest rates to savings accounts, but they are generally offered by brokerages and can come with debit cards or checks.

Best for: Savings accounts are best for short-term savings or money that you need to access only occasionally; think about an emergency or vacation fund. Savings account transactions are limited to six per month. Cash management accounts offer more flexibility and similar, or in some cases, higher interest rates. If you are new to the world of saving and investing, a good rule of thumb is to keep three to six months of living expenses in an account like this before spending more on the investment products further down this list.

Where to open a savings account: Due to lower overhead costs, online banks tend to offer higher rates than you would at traditional banks with physical branches. View our roundup of the best high-yield savings accounts to find one that meets your needs.

Where to open a cash management account: Investment companies and robotic advisers like Betterment and SoFi offer competitive rates on cash management accounts.

2. Certificates of Deposit

A CD is a federally insured savings account that offers a fixed interest rate for a defined period of time.

Ideal for: A CD is for money that you know you will need on a fixed date in the future (for example, a down payment on a house or a wedding). Typical durations are one, three, and five years, so if you're trying to safely grow your money for a specific purpose within a predetermined time frame, CDs might be a good option. However, it is important to note that to get the money out of a CD sooner, you will likely have to pay a fee. As with other types of investments, don't buy a CD with money you may need soon.

Where to buy CDs: CDs are sold based on the length of the term, and the best rates are generally found at online banks and credit unions. See the best CD rates right now based on term length and account minimums.

3. Money market funds

Money market mutual funds are an investment product, not to be confused with money market accounts, which are bank deposit accounts similar to savings accounts. When you invest in a money market fund, your money buys a collection of high-quality, short-term government, bank, or corporate debt.

Ideal for: money that you may need soon and that you are willing to expose to a little more market risk. Investors also use money market funds to hold a portion of their portfolio in a safer investment than stocks, or as a deposit of money for future investments. While money market funds are technically an investment, don't expect the highest returns (and highest risk) from other investments on this page. The growth of money market funds is more like the returns of high-yield savings accounts.

Where to buy a money market mutual fund: Money market mutual funds can be purchased directly from a mutual fund provider or bank, but the widest selection will be available from an online discount brokerage (you will need to open a brokerage account).

4. Government bonds

A government bond is a loan that you make to a government agency (such as the federal or local government) that pays interest on the loan to investors over a period of time, usually one to 30 years. Because of this constant flow of payments, the bonds are referred to as fixed income securities. Treasury bonds are virtually a risk-free investment as they are backed by the full confidence and creditworthiness of the US government. The disadvantages? In return for this security, you won't get as high a return on government bonds as you would on other types of investments. If you had a 100% bond portfolio (rather than a mix of stocks and bonds) it would be much harder to achieve your retirement or long-term goals. (For more information, see our bonus explainer.)

Ideal for: conservative investors who prefer less volatility in their portfolio. "Bonds weigh on a portfolio and generally rise when stocks fall. This allows nervous investors to stick to their investment plan and not panic," said Delia Fernández, certified financial planner and founder of Fernandez. Financial advice. in Los Alamitos, California. Fixed income and lower bond volatility make them common with approaching or retiring investors who may not have long enough investment horizons to deal with unexpected or severe market downturns.

Where to Buy Government Bonds: You can buy individual bonds or bond funds with a variety of bonds for diversification from a broker or directly from the insurance investment bank or the US government. Our Guide to Buying Bonds will help you identify which types to buy and where.

5. Corporate bonds

Corporate bonds work just like government bonds, except that you are lending to a company, not a government. Hence, these loans are not secured by the government, making them a riskier option. And if it's a high yield bond (sometimes called a junk bond), these can be significantly riskier if a risk-return profile is adopted that is more like stocks than bonds.

Ideal for: Investors who are looking for a fixed income security with potentially higher yields than government bonds and who are willing to take a slightly higher risk in return. With corporate bonds, the higher the likelihood that the company will close, the higher the yield. In contrast, the bonds of large, stable companies tend to underperform. It is up to the investor to find the right risk / return ratio for them.

Where to buy corporate bonds: Similar to government bonds, you can buy corporate bond funds or individual bonds through an investment broker.

6. Mutual Funds

A mutual fund pools cash from investors to buy stocks, bonds, or other assets. Mutual funds offer investors an inexpensive way to diversify by spreading their money across multiple investments to protect themselves from losses on one investment.

Great For: When you're saving for retirement or some other long-term goal, mutual funds are a convenient way to expose yourself to the superior investment returns of the stock market without having to buy and manage a portfolio of individual stocks. Some funds limit the scope of their investments to companies that meet certain criteria, e.g. B. Technology companies in the biotech industry or companies that pay high dividends. This allows you to focus on specific investment niches.

Where to Buy Mutual Funds: Mutual funds are available direct from the companies that manage them as well as through discount brokerage firms. Almost all of the mutual fund providers we reviewed offer no-transaction-fee (meaning no fees) mutual funds and tools to help you choose funds. Note that mutual funds generally require a minimum investment of between 500 and thousands of dollars, although some providers waive the minimum investment if you agree to set up automatic monthly investments.

7. Index funds

An index fund is a type of mutual fund that holds the stocks of a specific market index (for example, the S&P 500 or the Dow Jones Industrial Average). The goal is to achieve a return on investment that is in line with the performance of the underlying index, as opposed to an actively managed mutual fund that pays a professional to curate a fund's holdings.

Best for: Index mutual funds are some of the best investments available for long-term savings goals. Index mutual funds are not only less expensive due to lower fund management fees, but they are also less volatile than actively managed funds trying to beat the market. Index funds are especially suitable for young, long-term investors, who may invest more of their portfolio in equity funds with higher returns than more conservative investments such as bonds. According to Fernandez, young investors who can emotionally weather the ebb and flow of the market might do well to invest their entire portfolio in equity funds early on. Index Fund Supply Sources - Index funds are available directly from fund providers or a discount broker. Our post tells you how to invest in index funds.

8. Exchange-traded funds

ETFs are like mutual funds in that they pool investors' money to buy a collection of stocks to provide a single diversified investment. The difference is in how they are sold: Investors buy shares in ETFs in the same way that they buy shares in a single share.

Ideal for: Like index funds and mutual funds, ETFs are a good investment when you have a long time horizon. Additionally, ETFs are ideal for investors who do not have enough cash to meet the minimum investment requirements for a mutual fund, as the price of an ETF's shares may be below the mutual fund's minimum.

Where to buy ETFs: ETFs have ticker symbols like stocks and are available through discount brokers. (See our roundup of the best ETF investment brokers.) Robotic advisers also use ETFs to build client portfolios.

9. Dividend shares

Dividend stocks can enable fixed-income bond securities, as well as the growth of individual stocks and equity funds. Dividends are regular cash payments that companies make to shareholders and are often associated with stable and profitable companies. While the share prices of some dividend stocks may not rise as high or as fast as growing companies, they can be attractive to investors because of the dividends and stability they offer.

Best suited for: Any investor, from beginners to retirees. However, there are certain types of dividend stocks that may be better depending on where you are on your investment journey. For example, young investors could do well with dividend producers, which are companies that have a proven track record of increasing their dividends one at a time. These companies may not have high returns right now, but if their dividend growth continues, they could do so in the future. Over a sufficiently long period of time, this (when combined with a dividend reinvestment plan) can generate returns equivalent to those of growth stocks that do not pay dividends. Older investors looking for more stability or fixed income stocks might consider stocks that pay constant dividends. Reinvesting these dividends in a shorter period of time may not be the goal. Rather, taking dividends as cash could be part of a fixed income investment plan.

Where to Buy Dividend Stock: Like others on this list, the easiest way to buy dividend stock is through an online broker. For more information, check out our post on high-dividend stocks and how to invest in them.

10. Individual actions

A share represents a stake in a company. Stocks offer the highest potential return on your investment and the most volatility in your money. These words of caution are not meant to keep you away from stocks. Rather, they are designed to guide you towards the diversification that buying a collection of stocks through mutual funds provides, rather than buying them individually.

Ideal for: Investors with a well diversified portfolio who are willing to take a little more risk. Due to the volatility of individual stocks, it is a good rule of thumb for investors to limit their holdings of individual stocks to 10% or less of their total portfolio.

Where to Buy Stocks: The easiest, cheapest way to buy stocks is through an online discount broker. Once you've set up and funded an account, choose your order type and become a serious shareholder. Here are step-by-step instructions on how to buy stocks.

11. Alternative investments

Unless you are investing in the stocks, bonds, or cash equivalents listed above, your investment is most likely in the alternative asset class. These include cryptocurrencies, gold and silver, private equity, hedge funds, and even coins, stamps, alcohol, and art.

Alternative investments became increasingly popular in the years following the Great Recession, when both shareholders and bondholders saw their savings plummet. For example, gold prices rose in 2011 and reached highs that only collapsed in August 2020. However, this is part of the alternative investments course as these often unregulated instruments are volatile.

Ideal for: Investors (in many cases accredited investors) who deviate from traditional investments and want to protect themselves from price falls on the equity and bond markets.

Alternative Investment Sources: While some online brokers offer access to certain alternative investments, most alternatives are only available through private wealth management companies. However, there are ETFs such as gold and private equity ETFs that replicate the asset itself, as well as companies that are related to the asset (such as gold mining and refining companies).

12. Real estate

Traditional real estate investments involve buying and later selling a property for a profit or owning a property and collecting rent as a form of fixed income securities. But there are many other ways to invest in real estate, much more without intervention. A common route is through real estate mutual funds or REITs. These are companies that own income generating properties (like shopping malls, hotels, offices, etc.) and offer regular dividend payments. Real estate crowdfunding platforms, which often pool investors' money for investments in real estate projects, have also gained popularity in recent years.

Ideal for: Investors who already have a healthy investment portfolio and are looking for greater diversification or are willing to take more risks in order to achieve higher returns. Real estate investments are very illiquid, so investors shouldn't be investing in the money they may need to access quickly.

How to Invest in Real Estate: Some REITs can be bought on the public exchange through an online stockbroker, while others are only available in private markets. Similarly, some crowdfunding platforms are only open to accredited investors, while others have no restrictions on investment opportunities.

CHAPTER 13

HOW TO OPEN A MARIJUANA

DISPENSARY

---

1. Assess your commitment and eligibility

Lincoln Fish moved into the medical marijuana industry to challenge the hypocrisy. "He was with most of the people. I thought, 'It's drugs, this is bad,' "says Lincoln. "Then you start to learn how much hypocrisy surrounds marijuana. Alcohol and tobacco are much more harmful, much more addictive. Schedule 1 Narcotics by legal definition are highly addictive, have been shown to have no medicinal benefits, and can be harmful to the point of lethality. Alcohol and tobacco meet all three requirements, and marijuana meets none. "Mitch Woolhiser saw a magnificent and unusual business opportunity in the fledgling marijuana industry in 2010." This is something that, as an entrepreneur, you can do. And it's almost revolutionary, "he says." It's the chance of a lifetime. What product suddenly becomes legal that hasn't been for a long time? Something like this hasn't happened since alcohol prohibition and probably won't be happen in my life. " But Mitch and Lincoln caution against opening a dispensary solely for financial gain. "If the only reason you're getting into this is for money, you're not going to have a good time," says Mitch. "It's not a 'get rich quick' plan. It's a long game. You have to have something else to motivate you." It's also important to recognize that background checks are often required, not just for the owner of a dispensary, but also for investors and employees. If you have a criminal record, you may not be eligible to open a dispensary.

Also, if medical marijuana is not legalized in your state, any dispensary can be closed by the federal government. If there are no laws or regulations in your area, opening a dispensary is probably not a good idea. "If the city or county has not approved anything, then the state's default position is that there is nothing legal there," Lincoln says. "You have to be very careful. That could be a problem. They could shut it down." Considering the money you'll spend to open a dispensary, it's not worth the risk of trying to operate one illegally.

2. Investigate

The dispensary business is littered with legislation and regulation. For example, even determining how you will accept payments as a cannabis business is a tricky subject and something you'll want to think about a lot. To be successful as a dispensary owner, you need to understand not only the existing laws on growing and selling marijuana, but also the proposed laws and the changes that will take effect in the coming years. Lincoln Fish recommends reading Cole's Memorandum, which provides guidance to US state prosecutors on how to prioritize enforcement of marijuana laws. If he's in California, he also recommends reading Proposition 215 and Proposition 420. "In most cities and counties, it's very easy to study and see what the legislation is," Lincoln says. "Either it is totally prohibited [or] if it is not, they have already issued ordinances and guidelines."

The National Organization for Marijuana Law Reform, or NORML, has a database of detailed marijuana laws and penalties for all US states. These charts from the National Conference of State Legislatures are also helpful. . "There are many rules to follow and I highly recommend that people get help early on - an attorney and a certified public accountant," Lincoln says. This will help you comply with the law and access permits and licenses. NORML has a database of attorneys from across the United States who specialize in the marijuana industry. Both Mitch and Lincoln recommend a rigorous study of US Code 280E, a complicated tax code that can mislead dispensary owners, especially in budgeting.

"If he's dealing with a Schedule I narcotic, which is marijuana, he can only deduct the cost of goods sold from his income before doing his taxes," Lincoln explains. "Let's say you buy the product for $ 500, put it on the shelf, and sell it for $ 1000. You would have to pay taxes on a $ 500 profit before you can withdraw your rent, employees, etc. What is happening to many dispensaries is that they are filling up with huge tax bills. This is another reason why opening a dispensary is not necessarily as lucrative as people think. "

3. Find a rental property

"The key really is to find property that meets the standards," says Lincoln. In San Diego, a qualifying property has many requirements: "To be a compliant property, it must be more than 1,000 feet from a church, 1,000 feet from a school, 1,000 feet from a residential area, and 1,000 feet from another compliant property. " says Lincoln. "There is an online map that lists all properties that meet San Diego County's standards." It is important to remember that due to the ever-changing environment for marijuana, a property that is now compliant may not exists two years. "Make sure that when you access a property, you comply with the new laws that will go into effect in 2017, 2018," says Lincoln. "Make sure you don't open and close any, as this is against new laws. "A compliant property means different things in different places and even if you do find a compliant property you should be honest with the owner about what you are going to do about opening a pharmacy there and it may not be supported. Mitch Woolhiser saw this when he was looking for space for his pharmacy in 2010. "Some owners just didn't want to bother with it, and still don't want it," says Mitch. "Part of that is down to federal illegality and the responsibilities they have could."

Homeowners are sometimes pressured by law enforcement agencies. Mother Earth Collective, which previously operated in what is now the Outliers Collective in San Diego, has been indirectly ousted by the DEA. "The DEA sent letters to landlords across the country saying, 'Hey, if we decide to attack these guys, you may be held accountable for renting them.' The owner kicked them out and closed the bus. Lincoln explains. If you're looking for a place to open your pharmacy, consider whether that is suitable for potential customers. "For planning purposes, location is the most important thing to do retail. "says Mitch." People come to you because it's a destination or because it's convenient. "Identifying a target market can help you choose a good location for your business. It's also important that the Most, if not all, members of your community (even) non-users who will not be your customers will feel comfortable in a local pharmacy.If your county or city has nominations for marijuana laws, Mitch recommends looking at the election results for access any area you are considering ownership.

"In Colorado, we had a vote in 2012 on Amendment 64, which is the Recovery Act," he says. "I went to the Secretary of State's website and got the election results from Edgewater [where the Northern Lights Cannabis Company is located]. At Edgewater it was 70 percent. You can find this information in another community. You can find out the results of these voting questions and use this information to decide whether or not the community is welcome. ""

4. Write a business plan

When an industry like the medical marijuana industry is saturated, it is even more important that you appear professional and are prepared with a solid business plan. Mitch, who created his pharmacy business plan with Bplans in 2010, says a business plan makes you stand out from the crowd. "Write a business plan," he says. "There are a lot of people involved in this business and they are not very serious. Understand what you are getting yourself into and don't listen to someone high in the sky."

Access to capital

Any good business plan starts with access to capital, which is one of the most difficult parts of the marijuana industry because it costs a lot. "The barriers to entry are still pretty high," says Mitch. "It will cost a lot more money than it used to be. We got into it with about fifty thousand dollars and some credit cards. Now he couldn't get on without at least half a million due to regulations. Also because there is a lot of competition ". Due to the state illegality of marijuana, you cannot get a bank loan for a pharmacy. Lincoln recommends sticking to personal resources for his seed capital. "You'd better focus on angel investors, friends and family now in order to get to the point where you can buy a property," says Lincoln. "Many investors will not speak to you until you have a lot of things under your belt. When you have a compliant property it gets easier. "

Determine your budget

Another consideration in your business plan is a clear and precise budget. "You have to budget and consider the 280E," says Lincoln. "You can't do that with very little money. You need to be prepared to grow slowly. "Inquire with the wholesalers in your area about the cost of the products." For the business plan itself, you need to know your cost in relation to the cost of getting the product, "he says. Mitch In addition to your product cost, there are other budget considerations:

- ➢ Rental costs
- ➢ License costs
- ➢ License application fee
- ➢ Employee salary
- ➢ Product transportation and storage
- ➢ security
- ➢ Research the competition

When opening a pharmacy, not only do you need to know the licensed competition in your area, but you also need to think about another competitive demographic that presents additional challenges: unlicensed operators. "Understand the landscape of unlicensed competition in this area," says Lincoln. "What are the law enforcement agencies doing about it or what are they planning to do? The truth is that the unlicensed are allowed to roam wild. The police are working to shut them down, but it's not a high priority as they can't get convictions. "Check local publications for ads for physical and delivery pharmacies. This will give you an idea of unlicensed operators in your area Investigate criminal robberies for unlicensed operations in your area. Are unlicensed pharmacies free or law enforcement working on them get rid of? This is good information to help educate your business plan.

Do market research

Your business plan provides an important opportunity to identify your customers. This is a great way to inform your pharmacy's marketing and pricing strategy. "Know your market," says Lincoln. Know your demographics and psychographics. Is there any consumer demand? Where is? This will also determine some of your prices. "

5. Get a license

Getting a license to open a medical marijuana dispensary is often difficult and expensive. "I've met people who spent more than three to four thousand dollars in legal fees to get their license," says Lincoln. For example, in Colorado, the registration fee for a medical marijuana dispensary can be as high as $ 15,000. "Be prepared to spend a lot of time on compliance and have plenty of resources to do so," says Mitch. "A lot has been consolidated here because many smaller companies cannot keep up with compliance. It's a full time job. "Check out Colorado's retail and medical marijuana license application process to get an idea of what your application process would be like.

6. Receive product

Getting a good product for your marijuana pharmacy and making sure you do it legally is a key part of starting a successful pharmacy. Many pharmacies grow their own marijuana, and some states require it. Mitch Woolhiser has his own grow facility for the Northern Lights Cannabis Company and says it should be on the horizon for any pharmacy owner. "Open a retail facility first, then keep an eye on your own growing facility," he says. "Bring wholesale retail to market. I would recommend it. "Opening a pharmacy doesn't mean you have to sell marijuana in its typical form. Many patients prefer foods, oils, touches, and concentrates. Mitch says sellers of these forms of marijuana are easy to find and do business with." When it comes to groceries and concentrates, these companies have sales reps, "he says." Just get in touch and get in touch with them.

7. Market your pharmacy

Decide what makes your pharmacy competitive and sell it. "You can compete on price or other things and I chose other things," says Mitch. "We are trying to be more of a boutique. For us, you ask all the questions, you can smell and look at each type before deciding to buy. Create a more unique shopping experience. "Outliers Collective also targets a more mature audience. "We look for long-term customers who come to us because they want service, quality and consistency," says Lincoln. "We want to attract a different type of patient, people who take care of all the things that are a licensed place." Your target market will inform some of your marketing decisions, but Lincoln says there are some must-haves to marketing your new pharmacy. "You have to be on

Weed Maps and Leafly," he says. Weed Maps and Leafly are apps that patients can use to find pharmacies in their area. Lincoln also uses some magazine ads and has a billboard on California State Route 67. Mitch recommends marketing through social media accounts like Instagram, encouraging customers to leave reviews on Google, and keeping your website up-to-date with the proper SEO strategies to stay on track. Both Mitch and Lincoln use loyalty programs that allow them to orally market their pharmacies. A program that gives customers credit when they refer a new customer expands your customer base.

CHAPTER 14

CANNABIS INDUSTRY

The "cannabis industry" refers to all activities and professionals that are directly or in a secondary or tangential role involved in the manufacture, transport, sale and legal consumption or use of medical marijuana, recreational marijuana and hemp and all derivative products from them. are theirs. It includes healthcare workers, legal professionals, legislators, pharmacy owners and employees, farmers and farmers, individuals and companies that make products that use oils and seeds for health and beauty products, and all those involved in their transportation and handling. are. As a legal industry, it has only existed in the modern world from the mid to late 1990s and has grown exponentially since the early 21st century.

Given this increasingly favorable global framework for the legal production and sale of cannabis derivatives, the cannabis industry sees a huge potential market worth billions of dollars. Some estimates even put the cannabis industry at an annual growth rate of 16% for the next few years, so this business is expected to generate sales in 2,025 on par with the current sales of a giant in the cannabis industry. . Fashion like Inditex. These growth expectations for the sector, comparable to those generated by dot-com companies, have not gone unnoticed by the large investors of the first decade of this century. Highly respected business magazines such as Forbes or highly influential financial and business sector agencies such as Bloomberg have already dedicated numerous articles to the cannabis industry, offering such a great opportunity to generate a significant return on investment. Large fortunes such as PayPal co-founder Peter Thiel or Corona beer owner have largely relied on this emerging industry and provided a boost for other large holding companies, including the banking, construction sectors. and metal. For example, the share price of some medical cannabis producers has shown a much higher growth rate over the past year than that of traditional sectors or new technologies. The traditional pharmaceutical industry has not escaped this boom in the cannabis sector either. Large pharmaceutical companies have forged strategic alliances, mainly with Canadian companies, world pioneers in the sector, to take over the market for the manufacture and distribution of cannabis preparations for therapeutic purposes.

The cannabis industry is made up of legal growers and producers, consumers, independent industry standards, ancillary products and services, regulators and researchers related to cannabis and its industrial derivative, hemp. The cannabis industry has been constrained by regulatory restrictions for most of its recent history, but the legal market has developed rapidly as more governments legalize adult and medicinal use. Uruguay was the first country to legalize marijuana in Uruguay through legislation in December 2013. Canada became the first country to legalize the private sale of recreational marijuana in Canada with Bill C-45 in 2018.

Globally, the marijuana industry has grown tremendously as more and more countries legalize cannabis. The market shows no signs of slowing down, and industry analysts expect the global market for legal marijuana to grow from its current value of $ 9.2 billion to a staggering $ 57 billion by 2027.

As an emerging industry, individuals and businesses involved in the cannabis trade are still going through various hurdles and bureaucracies that have not kept pace with the changing laws and attitudes regarding legal cannabis, or that were not designed from scratch to the beginning. final. rather, the only framework is present in some places. The industry still lacks some of the basic amenities that other companies take for granted, such as access to banking institutions and national legal protection. In some cases, the laws will be updated; in other areas, innovators in the cannabis industry are taking a new path, for example with electronic currency specific to cannabis transactions or with numerous platforms that are supposed to connect consumers to products without using commercial channels traditional.

MINOR MISTAKES THAT WILL RUIN YOUR CANNABIS BRAND

1. BAD LOGO DESIGN

Your logo design can make your business fail! If they are too busy, they can appear childish and unprofessional. If your logo is too boring or generic, you can get lost in the sea of brands that consumers face every day. Hiring a professional graphic designer or business is the best way to give your business a unique and memorable logo that will stand out from the crowd.

2. LOW QUALITY IMAGES

How would you feel if you researched a company and all the images were blurry or pixelated? You are probably not very confident! Poor quality images are one of a potential customer's first red flags that your business may not be as professional and trustworthy as you would like to believe. Do your best and invest in high resolution images!

3. CHEAP PHOTOGRAPH

Photography is a client preview for your business. When your images don't show how good your product or service is, people will switch to your competitors. It is tempting to take a photo yourself, but don't do it! Well-lit and carefully edited photos make a big difference when it comes to brand interest. Only a professional photographer can provide the quality, composition, and post-production necessary to create compelling photographs to get people interested enough to run your business.

4. FORGET THE BRAND

This may sound simple to you, but one mistake is all too common! If you don't establish a brand identity, your website, social media pages, business cards, brochures, etc. will have their own look and feel. How are people supposed to know your company from one place to another if it doesn't look like the same company? If you want brand awareness, you need to have brand consistency first. That means EVERYTHING your business uses needs to match, from color palettes and fonts to the overall layout composition. The more familiar your brand feels across all touchpoints, the more likely consumers will come back to you in the future.

5. OUTDATED WEBSITE

None of the above will help you much if your website is outdated or poorly designed. This is the age of technology and prospects will first see your website before you have a chance to speak to them. An outdated, ugly, or broken website will quickly turn people away from your brand. With nearly 72% of smartphone owners using their phone to search for businesses online, this can easily mean that shopping customers click through to your website and immediately leave to go elsewhere.

6. EXCELLENT PROMOTIONS

Promotions are great for generating quick interest and income spikes, but you have to be careful not to look too desperate! If your company runs "50% off" promotions on a regular basis, it will appear that you are just trying to get the business going. No one is going to take your brand seriously if you seem too eager to get a customer you can, in any way you can. Instead, promotions need to be relevant and still convey high value to the customer. That is not a value in terms of the money saved, but a value in terms of paying a fair amount for what they get in return.

7. CONTRIBUTION TO THE COUNTERCULTURE

Medical cannabis and recreational cannabis are currently legal in several states, so it's ridiculous that cannabis brands should continue to cling to black market culture. Instead, we should seek high-level ideals that help make cannabis look and function like a legitimate industry. Your cannabis brand needs to be able to relate to the main market. Now thousands of other brands of cannabis go head-to-toe so there's no point wasting time looking sticky.

8. SHARE BY SHARE

Nobody wants to be "that account that I didn't have to follow anymore because my feed was bombed. When it comes to social media, a good rule of thumb is this: if you don't have anything relevant to say, don't say anything! Good, quality content is far more important than the frequency with which you post. So, if you're not telling your followers something that's really worth it, you're doing your brand a disservice.

9. NEGATIVITY / ATTITUDE

Do you want your brand to be highly respected by consumers? Keep your mood. There will be people, reviews, and other business owners who will test your patience. No matter how tempting it may be to react sarcastically or defensively to them, make sure you and all of your staff react as gracefully as possible! The moment you show an indication of a bad attitude, your brand is descending a slippery slope that looks awkward and unprofessional.

10. EXCESSIVE PROMISERS AND STANDARD

No matter how many amazing things you've done for them, customers can have surprisingly vivid memories when it comes to what your business did that they didn't like. Do not exceed your ability to meet expectations. This includes exaggerated results, undue promises in service, or preparing customers for features or products that have failed and / or never made it to market. It's easy to promise the world, but once you do, that's what customers will expect. So set realistic goals. Not only will you get positive feedback for meeting your deadlines, but if you take it a step further, your customers will be much more likely to direct your compliments to anyone who meets them.

MISTAKES TO AVOID WHEN MARKETING CANNABIS

Creating unrealistic expectations

Inexperienced entrepreneurs look to the cannabis industry and assume that marketing is booming and growing, and is a fail-safe investment. This could not be further from the truth. Entering a saturated market requires a significant commitment to the product or business and a great understanding of both the industry and the regulations. What may seem like a foolproof business plan could be completely solved with a legal error. Furthermore, a business plan without passion or knowledge of the industry can easily fall behind in the saturated market of cannabis aficionados who literally eat, sleep, and breathe cannabis. Be passionate about the company you are starting or investing in and have realistic growth expectations. While the cannabis industry has great potential for successful ventures, it cannot do without its fair share of complications.

Suppose other companies are willing to work with you.

Even in recovering countries, cannabis-related products and companies face constant obstacles to any operational effort. Dime Bags manufactures protective glass transport bags and uses hemp to make the fabric for our products. The bags arrive at our already built warehouse in Colorado Springs. There is no raw hemp in our building and there is certainly no cannabis on the premises, but we have faced setbacks and setbacks from many companies. We have been turned away by insurance companies, have had a difficult time finding a bank, and have even experienced direct bribery from the surrounding store fronts for the product we manufacture and market. Don't expect others to always welcome you with open arms, even if you are starting a business in a state of recreation. Do proper research beforehand with banks, accounting firms, lawyers, insurance companies, the location of your business, and any other possible associations to find those who support cannabis companies and are willing to work with them. As long as cannabis remains illegal across the country in the US, commercial cannabis companies will be turned away by other industries that are unwilling to take the risk. However, as public awareness shifts and more states become legal, there has been a notable increase in cannabis-friendly side businesses, and it is no longer entirely impossible to find the right association.

Do not adjust

As with starting a business, a lack of adaptation will cause your business to fail. In an industry where everyone is trying to break into while it's on the rise, the impact is ten times greater. The cannabis industry is constantly changing with the growing market. If you are not fully committed to adapting to the industry, your business will fail. With the cannabis industry still so new and not yet global, changes in behavior, attitudes, interests and trends are changing rapidly. Stay up-to-date with the latest industry discoveries to stay one step ahead of the curve for the "next big thing." Understanding the facilities themselves and the interests of consumers can help you spot trends before they take off. While Dime Bags originally only made hemp bags, we have expanded our range to include odor-proof technologies as we have recognized consumer demand. While having a vision and roadmap for your brand is important, you need to be open to changes in the marketplace and keep track of trends so you can make changes before the rest of the industry.

Break the law

While a thorough understanding of state and federal regulations is a crucial part of any cannabis business, breaking the law goes beyond day-to-day operations. Pay special attention to how your employees and your company behave. While your business may operate in compliance with state laws, this doesn't always protect you from random searches or anonymous suggestions made to regulators. If your company is hosting a launch party or industry event, ask yourself whether it is worth losing your local business. That's not to say that your state's laws can't do this, but an underage person caught smoking or someone enjoying a joint on the front door of your business could mean serious trouble for you. Clearly define your expectations for your employees, including their behavior at industry events, and define laws and regulations for everyone so you have a solid understanding of what is legal.

No backup plan

As Benjamin Franklin famously quoted, "If you fail to prepare, you are preparing to fail." Part of working in the cannabis industry is constantly preparing for the worst. Always have a backup plan when executing your strategy. The city can revoke an approval for an event that you sponsored for public reasons. Your packaging may not comply with the new legal requirements. The possibilities are endless. While it is impossible to predict all the problems that will arise, you have the capital to tackle difficult situations and plan alternatives before it's too late. As a rule of thumb, you need to save at least three months of operating costs to compensate for unexpected situations.

Take advantage of all the gaps.

Sometimes in this industry it is better to ask forgiveness than permission, but taking short cuts can result in breaking state or local laws that will end the business. Not all loopholes in state or local regulation are worth the risk, and you should take a high-level risk assessment by determining when to step on the gas and when to give in so the state can catch up.

Don't make education a priority.

With legal cannabis fast becoming the norm, it's easy to forget that this industry is still very new. There are still many unknowns about cannabinoids and their effects on the body, but as professionals who work with cannabis every day, you and your staff know the subject far better than most of your clients. Sharing what you know about your cannabis marketing strategy through social media, your website, or even through events hosted by your company can help spread awareness about cannabis and establish your company as an expert in its field. By publishing accurate information, it is possible to improve education and contribute to changing public perceptions, gradually reducing the remaining stigma.

CHAPTER 15

FINANCIAL PROBLEMS WITH

CANNABIS

Marijuana companies often (though not always) sit on piles of cash. Whether it's a warehouse growing the plant or a retail store selling it, cannabis companies are forced to do their business with physical bills as many banks and credit card businesses, including Visa, MasterCard and BECU, the largest credit union operating in Washington, refuse to work with them because the market is still illegal under federal law. This rejection puts everyone involved, from entrepreneurs to workers, at risk and prevents potential economic growth.

Just getting a license to run such a business could cost a lot in government fees and legal assistance, Katz said. "Make sure you have a source of money that is willing to raise capital in the pool when needed," he says. The marijuana banking ban also means difficulties in keeping money. However, some marijuana companies are finding ways to work around this problem. "Use a generic sounding name," says

Ean Seeb. That said, unless you add obvious adjectives like "green," "happy," or "psychedelic" to your cannabis business, bank tellers may turn a blind eye. However, joining a financial institution does not mean that you can rely on it. Seeb said how a bank he had worked with for four years suddenly emptied his company. "Don't get complacent," he says. "Open multiple accounts. So if the inevitable happens, you are ready to go into business."

Compliance with laws regulating legal marijuana can also cost more than it would for people in more secular industries. Joe Stevens, the founder of Greenleaf Compassion, New Jersey's first functioning pharmacy, didn't expect how expensive his operation would be. IRS Code 280e prohibits individuals engaging in illegal federal activities from writing off their expenses. Stevens is therefore forced to pay a 39 percent tax on all of his earnings, one of the highest rates in the state, without deducting normal business expenses.

The marijuana market has to cross a difficult line between regulation that discourages amateurs from engaging in large-scale drug production and control that is not so tight that entrepreneurship is discouraged. In Colorado and Washington, high up-front fees and an extensive licensing process ensure professionalism, but the lack of a good financial structure is damaging what may be America's next big growth industry.

In September last year, Bank of America announced that it would accept Washington State's marijuana tax revenues, even though the money is dirty in the eyes of the federal government. Credit cards like Visa and MasterCard still don't work with cannabis companies, but some pharmacies are finding ways to accept plastic through ATM-like systems to improve safety and convenience for workers and customers alike. Representatives of the Colorado and Washington House, Ed Perlmutter and Danny Heck, introduce the Commonsense Marijuana Business Access to Banking Act, which "aims to give financial institutions the assurance that they can make their own business decisions related to legal and financial transactions without To be afraid of government sanctions or criminal prosecution. "The law would open the way for more financial institutions to accept cannabis cash. However, it takes a lot of determination to build a legitimate business in this illicit form of drug trafficking. Founders need to be aware that the worst can happen, whether it means being attacked by crooks or the government - or both.

CANNABIS VALUATION

Fully legalized states allow adults 21 and over to purchase cannabis products from licensed recreational use pharmacies. Medical states allow cannabis products to be legally purchased from a pharmacy with a prescription, and decriminalized states (or cities within states) prohibit the possession, sale, and cultivation of large quantities of cannabis, but do not consider possession of one. small amount as a crime. to be.

Recreational cannabis legalization is a major advance in Canada and some states in the US that is attracting the attention of many top investors as cannabis stocks grew exponentially, outperforming major indices and other sectors starting at 2016. Legalization in the cannabis industry also presents huge opportunities for large companies to gain significant share of the global market through mergers and acquisitions. The cannabis industry is poised for considerable consolidation, and the resurgence we've seen in recent years is probably just the beginning. More and more mergers and acquisitions have placed increasing importance on transparent and robust company valuations in this industry.

Selling a product classified as a Schedule I drug by the federal government means that cannabis companies do not have widespread financial support from banks and financial institutions, nor can they deduct normal business expenses from their federal taxes. These restrictions call into question the expansion of the cannabis market in the United States. However, some states are addressing these challenges by allowing companies like cannabis credit unions to boost investment in the industry. A challenge to the growth of the industry is the market valuation in the largest publicly traded cannabis companies. Overly optimistic forecasts on cannabis growth predicted a rapid and expansive legalization of recreational activities in the US The fact that the pace has not lived up to expectations and the slow rollout of the Canadian market is leading to analysts to now revise the forecasts to more realistic levels, which has caused a drop in the valuation of existing cannabis companies. However, cannabis companies continue to attract investment and capital, although market forecasts and valuations have fallen and capital investment still poses a risk, while cannabis remains a Schedule I substance under US federal law. According to Viridian Capital Investors, the cannabis industry reached $ 14 billion in 2018, a four-fold increase compared to 2017.

VALUATION APPROACHES FOR CANNABIS
1. Asset approach
2. Income approach
3. Market focus

1. ASSET APPROACH

An asset-based approach, sometimes called a cost-based approach, is a valuation technique that focuses on the adjusted net asset value, which is determined by subtracting the fair value of the company's assets and liabilities. There are two methods of the asset-based approach, namely the net settlement method and the net asset value method.

The net liquidation method calculates the value of the business based on the expected income at the time of liquidation of the company's assets as part of the company's dissolution. The method is often used when the business is not consistently profitable and the best value can be obtained by selling the underlying assets.

With the net asset value method, all of the company's assets and liabilities are adjusted to their fair value or "economic value" and their difference is determined. A valuation analyst may also use the cost of manufacturing or replacing the asset, minus a provision for obsolescence and physical depreciation.

Within the cannabis business, the asset approach is best suited in the following situations:

> ➢ The company is in operation.
> ➢ The value of the company depends largely on the value of its tangible assets.
> ➢ The company has little or no identifiable intangible assets.
> ➢ The balance sheet reflects all of the company's assets
> ➢ A business that operates at a loss with the expectation that there will be losses in the future too.

2. INCOME APPROACH

The income-related approach is based on the theory that a company's intrinsic value is based on expected future profits or income discounted at a reasonable rate of return that reflects the company's expectations of market return and the conditions of the company's market, the inherent cost of risk and opportunity in the market Investment. The earnings-related assessment method requires the following inputs:

> **Net Cash Flow Projections**: Financial projections of the amount of money the company will produce after paying all capital and operating costs.

> **Discount rate:** Refers to the cost of capital / return used to determine present value

> **Ending Value:** This is the value of the deal at the end of the projection period.

The two methods of income-based approaches that are mainly used are the Future Capitalized Earnings Method and the Discounted Future Earnings Method.

With the CCF method (Capitalized Cash Flow), the value of the transaction is determined by dividing a cash flow that is considered representative for the future for a period by the capitalization rate (capitalization rate).

The discounted future earnings method uses projections of the company's earnings and discounted them to the present using an appropriate discount rate.

3. MARKET FOCUS

The market approach involves determining the value of a company based on prices and goodwill multiples derived from the deal and selling similar deals to that company. There are two main types of market approaches used by valuation analysts: the guide's transaction method and the guide's business method.

The Guideline Company method compares the company in question with similar publicly traded companies: Applying the market approach to the valuation of a cannabis business presents valuation analysts with various challenges as there is limited market data available in the EU cannabis space. Although the market data has surfaced as the cannabis industry has grown in recent years, it is still a long way from becoming a mature industry. In addition, there are significant differences in case law in the cannabis industry, such as: B. Tax burdens, licenses, socio-political environment and state and local regulations. For example, some states in the United States have legalized medical marijuana and recreational marijuana, while some states only legalize medical marijuana. Similarly, cannabis is legal in Canada, so the Canadian business environment is more cannabis-friendly than the US.

The multiple most frequently used in the market approach is the enterprise value (EV) of earnings before interest, taxes, depreciation, and amortization. The table below shows the financial data and respective multipliers for the top 10 Canadian cannabis companies. As of August 2019 there is huge variability in multipliers. EV / LTM sales are between 7.2x and 175.7x and EV / LTM EBITDA between -13.2x and -186.5x. Most comparable companies have low or negative operating profits due to low sales and high operating costs. Most of the companies in the cannabis industry are in the early stages and are making significant operational investments to meet anticipated future demand and gain market share. A multiple due to historical low profitability indicates less than expected future growth due to recreational cannabis legalization and other opportunities for global expansion. Therefore, it makes sense to use prospective multiples when evaluating cannabis. This is the price paid today that reflects the expected financial future of tomorrow's business. Average EV / forecasted sales in 2021 are 7.1 times versus average EV / LTM sales of 72.7 times. Similarly, 2021 average EV / Projected EBITDA is 79.1 times compared to an EV / LTM average EBITDA of -68.0. Forward-looking multipliers are believed to result in a more reliable and logical assessment than using traditional multipliers for public companies. An alternative approach is to use market multiples of similar but more mature industries that are considered more comparable to cannabis, such as alcohol and tobacco, to determine the value of a mature market.

Policy, the transaction method compares the company in question with similar companies acquired or merged within reasonable proximity of the valuation date: it can be difficult to find comparable transactions and significant market multiples for the valuation of cannabis. Similar to the policy company method, most of the target companies are growing with the policy transaction method and have low or negative profitability. Therefore, this leads to negative multiples that are too high or negative. In the table below, the average EV / LTM implicit sales multiplier is 400.6x and the average EV / LTM implicit EBITDA multiple is - 37.5x.

CHAPTER 16

CANNABIS AUTOMATION

Automation in the enterprise is a smart way to alleviate tasks that can trigger growth, innovation and productivity for everyone involved. More than an expense, it is an investment, whose initial step is the conceptualization of what you want to achieve; The first investment in automation for growth is the will to do it. Then come all the technical, administrative, organizational, and human aspects of implementing automation. In fact, the concept of automation can and does not apply to how many things need to be improved, but to improve something you must first measure it. From cultivation to extraction or processing to sale, cannabis technology has succeeded in automating every aspect within the cannabis industry. Marijuana automation technology is perhaps one of the fastest growing sectors of the cannabis industry. This burgeoning market is not only limited to large-scale industrial operations, but also provides solutions for small producers who want to reduce their workforce while increasing efficiency and control over their crops. When growing at home for personal use, there are many reasons to use automation. For some, more control is the key. Others wish to farm without high supervision. No matter the budget or the number of plants, there are many ways that home growers can use automation technology in their crops, and surprisingly, many solutions are quite simple and inexpensive. Here are three ways you can take your growing to the next level with automation.

As the marijuana industry matures and evolves, wholesale prices for cannabis are plummeting in some markets, especially those that allow tens or hundreds of grow operations. The result: producers in these states face new competitive and financial pressures. Profit margins are shrinking, cannabis is becoming a commodity, and the big players are beginning to pressure their smaller counterparts by building economies of scale. These trends are particularly acute in the recreational market, but are also manifesting in medical cannabis states. And they are expected to accelerate in the coming years as the industry progresses. In the future, producers who do not or cannot adapt to these changes will be eaten up or completely destroyed by competition. Against this backdrop, growing companies are increasingly turning to automation to cut costs, gain an edge over the competition, tighten control over the growing process, and improve efficiency.

Mechanization can accomplish many of the things that people now do manually, like turning up the thermostat or watering and feeding plants. If implemented intelligently, automation can save companies tens of thousands of dollars in the long run and improve plant quality. But diving headlong into automation blindly can be a big mistake. Producers must be selective about which processes they choose to automate, and they must remember to do numerical calculations, particularly when it comes to production costs. While automation can be a great solution for many situations, producers have been known to spend six-figure sums on technology that they ultimately don't need or that fails them. Trial and error is sometimes a given.

Growers have different views on what should and shouldn't be automated and how different technologies should be implemented. What they do have in common is how they make their decisions: they review their costs and the problems they are trying to solve, and they determine how mechanization can help. Producers who take this approach to automation are much more likely to be successful.

AUTOMATE CANNABIS CULTIVATION
TIMER

Timers are the first step in adding automation to your indoor growth. Timers can be used for multiple tasks, and switching from manual to automated control can be surprisingly inexpensive. A single basic analog timer can cost up to $ 10 and offers a variety of solutions when connected to lights, fans, pumps, and other air conditioning equipment. This is a perfect tool if you want to minimize the labor and reduce the time spent on repetitive basic tasks. A series of timers may not be enough to keep your growth unattended for long periods of time, but they can reduce the workload. Many timers contain multiple inputs so that more than one climate control can operate on an identical schedule. When setting up a grow with multiple lights and fans, these timing systems are critical to avoid having to keep the systems turning on and off. Digital timers are also perfect for more professional crops and allow multiple settings to be programmed over a period of time. For example, digital timers can program fans, pumps and CO_2

systems to run at set intervals without manual intervention.

CLIMATE CONTROL KNIFE

Indoor, greenhouse and hydroponic plants rely heavily on air conditioning to ensure smooth operation. There are digital autopilot environmental controls like the one pictured below that can not only monitor and control CO2, temperature and humidity, but also record and store harvest data. Devices like this are great for gathering information on temperature and humidity spikes / jumps, as well as VPD (Vapor Pressure Deficit) information so you can fully optimize the climate and meet the needs of your plants. Other types of meters include this continuous pH monitoring system that automatically monitors pH and conductivity (total dissolved solids) over time. This device constantly measures the acidity of your growing medium, as well as conductivity, to determine if your plants are receiving enough nutrients. Having this type of control over your harvest will save you a lot of time and allow you to know exactly what the weather is like without getting your hands dirty.

IRRIGATION AND FERTILIZATION SYSTEMS

Irrigation and feeding are a little more difficult to automate than the climate. In part, this is because individual plants within the same grow space may require different amounts of water and nutrients based on microclimate patterns, genetics, and a host of other variables. However, systems designed for self-sufficiency and water are often complex and expensive. However, they don't necessarily have to be. The automated system of irrigation and nutrient addition is known as "fertigation", a common practice in both professional open-air farming and greenhouse-controlled agriculture. This process basically optimizes all aspects of a feeding program by calculating and mixing nutrients directly through an irrigation system. There are several benefits to using fertigation, including:

> Better nutrient efficiency and precision

> Reduction of nutrient leaching

> Reducing water consumption.

> Requires less work

Fertilization systems often include both hardware (i.e., pneumatic injectors, positive displacement diaphragm pumps, drip irrigation devices) and software to fully control the dosage of nutrients in the irrigation system. Many companies offer complete systems with professional installation, although these services are often expensive and not a good solution for small manufacturers. There are many cheaper DIY solutions out there using equipment found at most garden centers. These most basic kits only require some sort of tank with a distribution pump attached to the plumbing systems that supply the nutrients. These systems work very well in smaller hydroponic systems as well as in flood and drainage systems.

NOTE: Automation for home growers can go well beyond automated counters, timers, and feeding systems. From individual plant growth trays to fully automated growth cabinets and more, the options keep growing. Some systems are even designed to be completely controlled by apps on your phone. Others include post-harvest drying and curing boxes that are designed to regulate the temperature and humidity of the harvested buds. And then there are the cutting machines that take care of the tedious task of manicuring and peeling the dried flowers.

REASONS TO AUTOMATE THE CANNABIS BUSINESS

Automation increases production.

By automating harvest and post-harvest processes, you save working hours, increase production and maintain quality. If you can't climb at the right time, operating overhead can be crippling. Companies cannot simply press the pause for growth, even in the COVID-19 crisis. Many companies have benefited greatly. They need to manage operational and infrastructure costs and had expansion plans before the crisis. Investment capital can also be more difficult to obtain in current circumstances. This makes many companies hesitate about their expansion plans. In difficult market conditions, larger companies tend to thrive because they can compete better and take over market share previously held by smaller companies. Automation enables an increase in efficiency that can lead to an advantage in this highly competitive market. If you can't scale at the right time or increase your productivity by reducing processing time, you can't keep up.

Automation allows you to control the quality.

How do you get the best price at the point of sale and achieve customer loyalty? Your final product must be consistent, the overall appearance of the flower must be of high quality, and the integrity of the terpenes must be preserved. Manufacturers can rest assured that by using automation in part of their production line or throughout their process, they will get the same result every time they move raw material through a particular machine. They standardize product control in much the same way that most other consumer product manufacturers would expect. This type of precision in production is now seriously gaining ground in the cannabis space and will be vital to competitiveness.

Automation means managing smaller employees. Automation enables companies to keep a small, well-trained workforce over the long term. This is more cost-effective, saves time in employee turnover and training, and is less time-consuming for production managers. It is expensive and time-consuming to recruit new seasonal employees. Automation minimizes this or, in some cases, makes it completely redundant - a huge benefit. If fewer workers touch the product, the risk of contamination is reduced. High quality stainless steel devices that are easy to clean and effectively sterilize make a big difference in the safe handling of products. Financial losses caused by human error are particularly difficult for small and medium-sized manufacturers to absorb. Automation minimizes that risk - a good thing in an industry affected by price changes, changes in regulations, competition, and other economic factors. If you are able to control your product handling, you are at least responsible for what you can control.

Automation of tightened security measures

As the cannabis industry continues to flourish, the value is skyrocketing, creating an urgent need for tough, formidable security methods. It is extremely important for growers, pharmacies, and even consumers to keep these valuable plants safe while growing. In fact, cannabis farms are switching to automated robots that work with other human security teams to protect crops to lock parameters and lock everything securely. These automated robots come from Hardcar Security and other tech security services getting into the cannabis industry before it's too late. Although the robots cannot replace an entire human team, security costs are minimized overnight. Instead, these robots work with a human security team to enable early detection of intruders. This allows an appropriate security guard to call the authorities or respond to the threat.

Automation leads to good decisions

The advent of automation has also made real-time data available. The technology is getting smarter as information can now be collected in real time along the automation chain. If you are able to track accurate weights and collect log-specific data, you can route higher value raw material into a specific production stream. With machine sorting, for example, you can easily see which raw material is too small to make a top-quality product so that it can be sent straight to extraction. This way you avoid the loss of waste products from front-of-stream processing that are still valuable. Pursuing efficiency and profitability at every stage of production is still a relatively new concept, but one that is vital for moving into the future.

Automation improves safety in the workplace.

By using automation in your manufacturing facility, you can create space between employees to promote social distancing and workplace safety. With the option of conveyors transporting products from one station to another, employees no longer have to work in close proximity to one another. This helps ensure that your employees feel safe and can concentrate on the task at hand. Automation ultimately creates a healthy workplace culture where employees know that their health and safety are valued. The new landscape of automated and socially distant production facilities will remain with us for some time. It will likely be persistent as the pandemic ends because of the many benefits.

Delivery straight to your door

With a few taps on your phone, you can now order cannabis or a cannabis product to be dispensed right at your door. This means that patients who otherwise had no access to a pharmacy or other cannabis store can now order the cannabis products they want and have them delivered to them. Those who hesitate to automate are concerned about the jobs ahead when everything is automated. On the contrary, these automated technologies for the cannabis industry are not meant to do anyone's job - they are meant to alleviate a serious pain point in the industry and improve efficiency for business owners everywhere.

CHAPTER 17

CANNABIS TAX

Since 2017, medical cannabis has been allowed to be prescribed by doctors in Germany in the form of finished drugs, flowers and extracts. The sale of medicinal products containing cannabis in Germany in 2018 brought in 83 million euros gross and the state budget itself. According to the extrapolation of the umbrella organization of pharmacists, taxes of over 13 million euros were levied. Since the demand for medical cannabis is steadily increasing, the pharmacists' association expects even higher tax revenues for 2019. According to calculations, Germany had already imported cannabis drugs worth around 52 million euros in June of the 2020.

At first glance, the main activities related to cannabis are: production (cultivation, conversion, labeling, packaging) and sale (distribution, sale, marketing and transportation); Since the above bill stipulates that specialized public and private entities must be created to carry out these activities and that their only business is cannabis, we can assume that the income from these activities will be subject to income tax.

When we talk about production and sales, we are talking about the provision of services and the disposal of goods. Hence, the collection of VAT on cannabis is included, but it is about the purpose of using cannabis, because if that is the purpose then it is pharmaceuticals and patent products under Article 2A of the VAT Act. They would be calculated based on the 0% tax. If cannabis is not used medicinally as indicated, it is subject to the applicable legal provisions with the possibility of adding certain digits to the number of the VAT Act.

The third tax that is speculated to be applied to activities related to cannabis is the IEPS. This refers to the fact that the other two legal drugs (tobacco and alcohol) are in the products that pay this tax. It is therefore easy to assume that cannabis pays IEPS for some of its activities. It is also important to check what corresponds to the importation of goods within the meaning of the above tax, taking into account the treaties, in order to avoid double taxation with the countries signed by Mexico and legal in these countries.

At the state level, there are additional tax charges for the sale of this product. For example, Colorado (with a population similar to Costa Rica) has a 15% sales tax on retail sales which, according to that state's Treasury Department, adds licenses and sales permits and brings in $ 247 million in additional income in 2017.

Uruguay, on the other hand, sees the question of legalization differently. The country that first legalized recreational marijuana use in Latin America will not levy indirect taxes on the sale of marijuana, and only a small portion of the profit margin from its marketing would go to the Institute for Regulation and Control of Cannabis (Operation). It is important to keep in mind that the entire production process is carried out by the same government, which is a distinct difference from the US. The intention behind this is to encourage regulated consumption and therefore its sale is not taxed at the specific internal tax as is the case with tobacco sales. Hence there would not be an increase in collection, but an eventual saving, as the resources for tracking sellers and consumers would decrease.

However, the most important thing about this cannabis taxation issue will be that the criteria by which these taxes are defined are geared towards the common good, the maintenance of public health, and not just about making profits, which is what applies. In this context, this broad proposal rightly provides for the creation of the Mexican Institute for the Regulation and Control of Cannabis, which would form an anonymous register and have an advisory council with the participation of the Treasury.

Taxes help state governments monitor their legal cannabis markets and ensure that revenues match a licensee's inventory. For example, a 2019 Nevada audit found that the information reported on tax returns did not match the information entered in the state's track and trace software. The state could then keep track of companies that reported discrepancies. Too many onerous tax tiers can undermine the cannabis market and pull consumers and businesses away from the unregulated market. When states legalize, they have to create new structures that do not force their residents into cheaper, unsafe and criminal market products. Without this balance - either local, state, or federal - the US will struggle to become an international leader in the burgeoning cannabis industry.

TYPES OF CANNABIS TAX

Business Tax

First, there is the business tax, which is a percentage of your profit. Business taxes, municipal taxes, or post-tax fees are determined by local governments. It is up to their discretion whether or not to apply this tax. Medical patients may be exempt from the local business tax or pay a lower tax rate than adult-use customers. All other industries can make tax exemptions on business expenses, making their taxable amount the net income after expenses. However, the Federal government still recognizes cannabis as an illegal substance, so these exemptions are not allowed for the marijuana sector. Yet, cannabis businesses are still taxed because they make a profit and it is their gross income that is subjected to federal taxation. Also, many states include a business tax that takes a percentage of the gross income. For example, Washington state has a business tax in addition to a sales tax on every transaction.

Excise Tax

If you are a distributor, your state may also apply an excise tax. This means you are taxed on the transfer of your product to a retailer or manufacturer. The tax amount is based on the retail market value of the product, which is calculated by the gross income of the product. This includes transportation, labor, other taxes, and sale price. The distributor is responsible for determining the value and collecting it from the retailer to include in their marijuana tax filing. All legal cannabis sales must include the excise tax which is collected quarterly by the state to be used for various initiatives such as mental health treatment, substance abuse programs, environmental efforts, and cannabis research.

Cultivation Tax

This taxing is based on the weight and type of cannabis entering the market from a cultivator. The tax per weight varies depending on the state standards. It also changes if the product is dried cannabis, untrimmed cannabis, or a fresh plant. Exclusions to this rule may be immature products, like clones, seeds, or plants that have not budded. It is the distributor's responsibility to collect the cultivation tax from the cultivator at the time of transfer. If it goes directly to the manufacturer, then they must collect the tax and pass it on to the distributor for filing.

Sales Tax

The most common type of marijuana tax revenue is per transaction called the sales tax. Each time a product is sold a percentage is added on to the total sale price. This is probably the easiest tax process since it is automatic. It is also the one type of tax that medical marijuana customers can be exempt from, but you, as the retailer, must still pay the taxes on the sale of products. The sales tax is the traditional tax we're all used to paying when we make purchases. The tax rate differs from state to state and city to city, usually it's between 4 percent and 17 percent. For example, the rate in Oregon is 17% while the sales tax in Montana is 4%. In states like California and Maryland, medical patients can avoid this tax with a valid medical marijuana identification card (MMID). Sales tax is added to the state's general fund and is often used towards public safety, health programs, local transportation, and education.

CHAPTER 18
IRS TAX CODE 280E

It's no secret that cannabis companies have a lot more rules and regulations to comply with compared to most other companies. Internal Revenue Code Section 280E is one of the biggest complications for companies operating in the cannabis industry, adding an increased tax burden for grow facilities, medical marijuana manufacturers, and pharmacies. Finding out which expenses are deductible and which are non-deductible under IRC Section 280E can help your cannabis business make better financial decisions. The IRS considers state-compliant cannabis companies illegal nationwide and requires that this be accounted for in federal tax returns. According to Section 280E of the Tax Code, companies that trade in controlled substances cannot deduct any costs incurred in the manufacture, distribution and sale of controlled substances. This means that companies operating in the cannabis industry are unable to deduct certain expenses, many of which are deductible for companies operating in a legal industry.

An exception to this law is the cost of goods sold (COGS). COGS are deductible and only take into account the costs associated with making the product. Deductible costs include items such as seeds, soil, water, nutrients, and costs related to growing and harvesting the plant. Expenses that are part of the sales process are non-deductible and include items such as rent, shipping, overheads, and employee expenses. As Section 280E deals with companies that concern only List I and II medicines, some companies have chosen to split their services and structure into two parts. The first company deals with the manufacture and distribution of cannabis, while the second is responsible for activities that are legal under federal law, e.g. B. providing care services or advice, selling related but non-marijuana fortified goods, and managing the place where the business is located. In this setup, the first enterprise conforms to Section 280E, so the cost of goods sold is the only allowable deduction. The second company has other common deductions related to payroll, rent, distribution, promotion, sales, support, administration, and management. Taken together, the taxes of the two companies are significantly lower than if they operated as a unit.

Most marijuana establishments are cash-based as mainstream national banking institutions are unwilling to support a nationwide illegal industry. A small number of government-chartered banks and credit unions have offered financial services for compliant operations, but building these relationships continues to be a major challenge for operators. An equally frustrating financial challenge is the IRS Tax Code 280E, which states that "There is no allowance or credit in running a business that consists of trafficking in controlled substances". This archaic code is affecting cannabis companies across the country, creating unnecessary tax and operational stress.

EFFECTIVE WAYS TO REDUCE TAX 280E
Determine the right corporate structure

There are three entity options when setting up your corporate structure: C-Corporation, S-Corporation, and Limited Liability Corporation (LLC). Most lawyers prefer a C Corporation structure for cannabis businesses in the middle of Section 280E, as it is a tax-paying entity. This means that the owner only pays taxes based on his wages or dividends. Meanwhile, S-Corporation and LLC are usually better for small businesses.

Consider the shared services agreement

Since Section 280E deals with businesses involving Schedule I and II drugs only, some companies chose to split their services and structure in two. The first company deals with the production and distribution of cannabis, while the second is responsible for activities that are legal under federal law, such as the provision of care or advisory services, the sale of related but not infused merchandise. marijuana and the management of the place where the business is developed. resides. Under that configuration, the first company complies with Section 280E, so cost of goods sold is the only deduction allowed. The second company, meanwhile, enjoys other ordinary deductions related to payroll, rent, distribution, promotion, sale, support, administration and management. When combined, the two companies' taxes are significantly lower than they would be if they operated as a single entity. This shared services agreement has been upheld by federal court in the 2007 case Californians Helping Alleviate Medical Problems (CHAMP). Be careful though - be sure to create a legitimate second business, with real purpose and income, to avoid breaches. Don't set up a shared services contract just to navigate through

Section 280E. Always check with compliance experts if you are unsure how.

Take note of employee tasks

Employee job descriptions are essential not only for having an organized internal process, but also for accurate reporting on wages. You should keep track of employee tasks and the time spent on each one to determine how many hours of wages are deductible under Section 280E of the tax code. For example, there may be cases where your grower works as a part-time budtender. The cultivation task is directly related to the production of cannabis. Therefore, it is deductible and is included in the cost of goods sold. Budget salaries, meanwhile, are not deductible.

Be prepared for audits

Your cannabis business is subject to more audits than other businesses, as it operates with an illegal substance at the federal level. Therefore, it is important to be prepared for an audit at all times. To deal with 280E and be ready for an audit, you need to document all expenses and income from planting and cultivation to marketing and sales. You should have a receipt for every transaction, even those involving the smallest invoice, to avoid filing an inaccurate tax return. Keep in mind that the IRS will ask for detailed documentation of your COGS, and you may face a penalty if you don't show how the deductions came to you.

Seek expert advice

Taxes and regulations, Section 280E in particular, can be confusing, and just one loophole could result in significant violations and fines. To avoid them, consider working with compliance and accounting experts. They can provide you with reliable information so you can make better business decisions. Accounting and compliance experts have advanced knowledge of the ins and outs of the highly regulated industry. They can help you stay calm and focused amid the Section 280E provision.

CHAPTER 19

HOW DO CANNABIS ENTREPRENEURS MANAGE?

Learn about local tax laws

Taxes vary not only by state, but also by county and city. It is very important to understand how these tax implications will affect your business before you familiarize yourself with automated tax calculations. It is best to check with an accountant to ensure accuracy and make the correct adjustments from there.

Set yourself up properly

Many entrepreneurs in the cannabis industry choose to start as a business for extra protection. The problem with Section 280E is that it does not allow deductions, creating what is known as "phantom income". This means that you will be taxed on money that you never see. A company protects business owners by creating a secondary business identity and helping them plan for additional tax burdens. Read more about it here.

Keep very detailed records

In order to comply with the strict compliance regulations, everything should be documented in detail. This includes every single issue from cultivation to marketing. Since a cannabis company is more likely to be affected by an IRS audit, you'll want to make sure you have a solid paper trail backing up your every move.

Categorize your employees

By categorizing the position of your employees in detail, you can avoid penalties by specifying the wages more precisely. By tracking each employee position and recording their time in each position, it will identify any actions that are deductible or non-deductible.

Create a tax code

Your tax responsibility as a business owner in this industry has levels. There are local taxes, state taxes, tax surcharges - you have the idea. Establish a procedure for applying these taxes to ensure the accuracy of your reports.

Be transparent

Due to geographic location and policies, taxes can vary by up to 15 percent on the same product. Make sure you are transparent to your customers on this to avoid complaints. You can do this by printing out the tax details on the product receipts, posting informational signs in your pharmacy, and making sure your retail staff can answer any customer questions.

Support your cannaprenuers

The reform of Section 280E will result in higher net income for everyone in the industry as well as the federal government. To break through tough federal regulations, everyone in the industry must work together for a 280E tax reform. So if your focus is on creating a strong community, there is enough for everyone.

CHAPTER 20

GROWING AND BECOMING A MULTI-LOCATION OR MULTI-STATE CANNABIS BUSINESS

The first thing to understand about MSOs is that the multistate carrier name is inappropriate. Various government operators would be a more appropriate name for the types of operations these companies perform. Multi-state gives the impression of a company shipping products from one state to another and going where it is needed. However, this is not the case. Federal law prohibits the transportation of state controlled substances across state lines. While cannabis remains in this class of substances, multi-state entities are in fact just a union of single-state operations and are denied the benefits of true multi-state operations.

The cannabis industry is in a fragmented state, dominated by small players from one state to another. Multi-state operators (MSOs), large, generally publicly traded companies with multi-state activities, will become more common in the cannabis industry as the space matures and more states relax restrictions. These companies develop and operate facilities for the cultivation, production, and retail of cannabis in virtually every state that has legalized cannabis for medicinal or recreational purposes.

This multi-state operating model also creates a huge duplication of effort. Most jurisdictions prefer or require vertical integration of cannabis companies. This means that if you establish yourself in a state with high consumer demand, you will have to purchase potentially expensive growing and production equipment that will add overhead and hurt your bottom line. A real multi-state operator could benefit from lower growing costs in one state to meet high demand in another state.

The increase in operators in various states is a consumer benefit in a complex and highly regulated industry and an expected development. Rather than having individual entrepreneurs start from scratch to discover operational efficiencies and conduct R&D on product formulations, MSOs generally have better access to capital, can more quickly establish facilities with proven designs and systems, and introduce a broader range of already developed products that can be produced cheaper than boutique operators. Many boutique dealerships are actively trying to get sucked into MSOs because the costs are overwhelming and the margins too low to do it on their own.

All business opportunities carry some degree of risk, but it is especially important that those in the cannabis room are aware of the potential dangers. Any marijuana business that wants to expand to multiple states must do it right. To do this, care must be taken to create the foundation and business structure for this growth. Although cannabis companies have been rated "important" in several states, the industry still lacks the rights, benefits, and safeguards necessary to do business successfully. Despite a fragmented market from state to state, several cannabis companies have outgrown their original location and expanded beyond their state borders. Operators who have reached this milestone often face a number of challenges for which there are no easy-to-prescribe solutions.

Due to the lack of federal legality for cannabis, the industry is limited in its domestic activities. Medical or adult use is legalized from state to state, and license applications are opened from state to state. However, interstate commerce is prohibited, which means that cannabis products grown in one state cannot be sold in another state. At the same time, the brand is important and medical cannabis is expected to at least be legal across the country within the decade. Therefore, it is a wise decision for cannabis companies to establish a brand that applies to several individual states and then can be expanded nationally to take advantage of the success and awareness of the brand.

When an MSO makes predictions about their sales today, they are in and of themselves based on the current expensive cost of cannabis. The high level of investment they are asking for is based on the expectation that cannabis will remain expensive. Even if the market stayed exactly where it is for five years in terms of case law, the price of consumer cannabis would still fall. Improvements in cultivation and production will lead to lower costs, and part of the competition will inevitably be lower prices. The more markets open up and more companies get involved in the cannabis industry, the faster it will happen. The industry will remain healthy as more consumers choose cannabis in all its forms at a lower price, but today's big MSOs, which rely on cannabis prices to stay high, are not doing as well.

PILLARS OF A MULTI-STATE CANNABIS BUSINESS

State license

The basic requirement for a multi-state marijuana business strategy is obtaining the state license in which you want to operate. Each state has its own regulatory and licensing scheme. This leads to large differences between states. That is why it is imperative to know the details. Point to one or more states where you can be licensed and study the state's residency and property requirements. Proactively anticipate which states are considering, or are about to consider, adopting a cannabis regulatory regime and prepare accordingly. Learn what it takes to get a license and whether the state is taking an open or closed market approach, offering limited licenses, or imposing a regulatory structure in which few licenses are issued. Understand each state's requirements for evidence of available financial resources, as this can sometimes be prohibitive. Most importantly, you have an experienced cannabis regulation and compliance attorney. Your services will be invaluable.

Get ownership

To expand to another state, suitable and qualified properties must be found and secured in which to establish your marijuana business. State regulatory restrictions on location, land use policies, and local zones can make it difficult to find a location that works for both the company and regulators. Negotiating the purchase or lease of real estate for a marijuana business is complex, time-consuming and, if not handled properly, involves unnecessary risk and cost. Every property has a story and that story can be fatal to your ambitions. Therefore, you want to work with an experienced real estate attorney who can alert you to liens, liens, easements, restrictions, contamination, and other factors that should influence your decision to buy (or not buy) a property. Even leasing real estate for a cannabis business is complex. Marijuana leases are unique. So simply using a standard lease or one provided by a landlord can cause problems. State regulators generally review any proposed lease or sublease as a requirement for obtaining a license. To ensure that your rental agreement not only includes the usual terms and conditions, but is also written to include custom and cannabis-specific terms, not only is a real estate attorney required, but one who is familiar is also required. with the marijuana laws and regulations of that state. family.

Adequate business structure

Having a reasonably flexible and adaptable business structure is important as a marijuana business expands to multiple states. A company or limited liability company incorporated and licensed in one state is certainly not qualified to be licensed in any other state. A multi-state marijuana company will have at least two or more licensed companies based in two or more states. Establishing separate entities for each section of a multi-state business operation provides certain safeguards, such as: B. Preventing the entire structure from collapsing if one section fails for some reason. If designed correctly, a multi-state marijuana company can use a general corporate structure that covers independent licensed companies, dividing the risk among the various subsidiaries. For example, in states that allow vertical integration, the owners can form a separate legal entity for both growth and retail. Different legal entities should also be considered for trademarks, trademarks and licenses, to own or lease real estate, and even for marijuana add-ons. The support of a legal advisor with experience in multi-state business law, tax law, and business training and structuring is vital. Correct structuring up front is smarter, cheaper, and easier than later repairs.

Access to the capital

As a marijuana business expands to multiple states, access to capital becomes a key business issue. In some cases, a state's licensing policy may require the company applying for the license to demonstrate significant financial resources. Capital for facility construction and business operations becomes critical. Most companies think about raising capital from investors. A company can raise capital by running into debt (borrowing money) or selling stocks (owned by the company). There are also areas where debt and equity overlap. For example, a company might offer convertible bonds that the holder can later convert into stocks. Once a company begins accepting money from outside investors, a variety of financial securities and regulations become important. This is especially true if your investors come from several countries. In addition to filing required by the Securities and Exchange Commission, each state has its own set of rules and filing requirements.

Also, note that not all investors are equally desirable. Knowing the rules for withdrawing funds from "accredited" versus "non-accredited" investors prior to accepting the investment can help you avoid violations, penalties and delays. Offering and selling any security (including debt) is a common business practice, but it requires caution and common sense. Before you get into trouble and climb out of a financial and / or legal loophole, get advice from a trusted attorney who has experience with securities and finance.

CHALLENGES AS A MULTI-STATE OPERATOR
Consistency

"Each market has its own specifics: how to advertise, the structure between wholesalers, brands and retailers, compliance rules, and how production facilities are managed to ensure products are consistent," explains Peter Barsoom, Director 1906 Executive, one of Colorado's most successful food companies. In late 2019, 1906 raised $ 18 million for its publication in Illinois, Massachusetts, and Michigan. When building a product brand, consistency of experience is key. That's why a Big Mac or Frappuccino tastes the same, whether you buy one in Boulder or Kalamazoo. This is inherently difficult to achieve with cannabis products, especially flowers, as the cannabinoid and terpene composition of the plant naturally varies with each batch. For a company that sells cannabis flowers and extracts, these challenges are exacerbated as it expands into new regions. "Consistency. That's the biggest challenge," says the former NBA player who became cannabis executive Al Harrington, CEO of Viola Brands. "The same strain in Colorado will be different in Michigan because of the environment. The regulations are country-specific, so we have to adapt to different cultivation techniques, production methods, regulations, packaging and sometimes THC limits.

Raising capital

Before a business can meet the challenge of creating new supply chains and reestablishing a coherent product line in new markets, it must first capitalize on its growth. Again, this presents unique challenges beyond the not-so-easy task of finding millions of dollars in investment capital. To control product quality and consistency, multistate operators often opt for vertical integration. This often leads to a structuring or restructuring problem in order to efficiently raise investor capital. "A multi-state operator has at least one entity for each state in which it operates. It can have several independent ones for each type of license. It is not uncommon for a multi-state operator to have 15 or 20 companies under an investment holding company means that it can have several different state regulators to approve remittances [if licenses are purchased] and each state has a different process for doing this, "explains Michael Harlow, CPA and partner who runs CohnReznick's cannabis practice." The real problem is that for the For most of these reorganization processes, you want the entire reorganization to occur at once as one transaction to qualify as a tax-free transaction. It is almost impossible to have government regulators from five or six different states with two or three licenses each. State to have to perform license transfers simultaneously approve. "

The difference can have millions of dollars in implications that can easily cripple a deal. Coordinating this type of transaction requires a deep understanding of compliance protocols in multiple communities and the ability to coordinate with multiple stakeholders.

Building a new customer base

After passing the myriad of examinations required to operate in a new state, a brand must return to the top spot to build a loyal and engaged customer base. Your California audience or population may not be relevant in Michigan. Illinois consumers can react completely differently to your messages, which worked so well in Colorado. Viola Brands has made a strategic move to address this piece of the puzzle by bringing in Ericka Pittman, a highly trained and experienced chief marketing officer, as CMO. When asked how Pittman plans to win in new markets, she shared her plan to "create brand equity by educating consumers. Cannabis is still a CPG. How do people choose dishwasher detergent? Is it very different from the way people choose cannabis products? "In keeping with Harrington's mission to" help as many people as possible through cannabis, especially those who look like me, "Pittman said," we want to lead community reinvestment and create social justice and economic access through we create educational opportunities. "Opportunities for extinction, opportunities for incubation and jobs."

Investing and engaging the local community is undoubtedly a proven way to build a loyal following. Another method is to influence the point of sale. According to Barsoom, "Budtenders are an integral part of the shopping and consumer experience, especially in emerging markets where people don't have much experience with legal cannabis. We focus on the formation of budget tenders. We have developed an extensive budget bidding training program that we can use in any region. "Most likely, brands Cathat thrive in multi-state businesses will have to invest resources in community engagement at the consumer, B2B and political level, as each state has its own ecosystem and culture.

Compliance

One entrepreneur's complex problem is another entrepreneur's business opportunity. The more brands that scale onto multi-state operations, the greater the potential to support them as they face the many challenges that come with that growth. "Outside the cannabis industry, manufacturers from several countries benefit from economies of scale. Although doing this is very difficult in the cannabis industry for a number of reasons, "said Julia Cortopassi, co-founder of Batch Bud, a software startup founded to help cannabis-infused manufacturers make their operations more efficient Scale Batchbud provides MSOs with a tool for coordinating the inventory of non-cannabis products across states for significant discounts on bulk orders and great traceability.

Cortopassi explains, "The government compliance software does not collect non-cannabis inventory. So let's say you are in Colorado and California and discover that many of the eggs you laid in a range of brownies in both states are at risk. If you have four hours by California standards to compile a list of everyone you've shipped these brownies to, you need to know which batches were affected quickly. It is very difficult to keep track of this without a tool like Batchbud, which is why the brand generally remembers all finished products from a certain date. It's a colossal waste of money and property. With Batchbud, companies can quickly and accurately regain compromised inventory in any market they expand into. "As the industry evolves, green entrepreneurs are smart to observe and uncover operational and regulatory inefficiencies for which they work can offer solutions on a large scale.

CHAPTER 21

CANNABIS PUBLIC RELATION

Cannabis companies and their leaders have struggled to leverage digital advertising to tell their story and increase brand awareness. Popular platforms like Google, Facebook, and Instagram aren't as cannabis-friendly as you might think. So in an age where content is king, what's the best move for a cannabis leader who works hard to tell his brand story, amplify awareness, build trust, and establish credibility as an industry expert? or option of choice in the B2B and B2C markets?

Public relations has proven to be a tremendous lever for leaders exploring ways to get around the rigorous digital advertising restrictions placed on the cannabis industry. When executed with precision, good public relations will put you in the driver's seat, allowing you to tell your story in a way that positions you and your brand the way it was intended to be presented from the moment it was who created it.

Cannabis is rapidly capturing attention. This booming sector is already worth more than $ 130 million in the

United States alone, according to the Hemp Business Journal. Major companies in the hemp industry are focused on sustained growth as changes are made in the legislature, as well as product development. Cannabidiol (CBD) products attract growing numbers of people, young and old, especially now that the 2018 Farm Bill has become law, legalizing hemp at the federal level.

As Louis Masensi and Cree Robinson, founders of touCanna put it, "The story of a new company deserves to be told in a way that clearly speaks to the founding team's passion, identity and vision for its clients. Public relations firms help introduce startups to the world by bringing their stories to life so people can see them from the eyes of a trusted source".

WAYS CANNABIS EXECUTIVES CAN BENEFIT FROM PUBLIC RELATIONS

1. Increase awareness

The precursor to increasing revenue is awareness. It doesn't matter how telling your story is or how revolutionary your product or service is if no one knows it's there. Franny Tacy, owner of Franny's Farmacy, explains, "A public relations professional is a critical, profitable role in a start-up like Franny's

Farmacy with such strong appeal, promise and history "She also advises all founders" be unforgettable and target a core audience. Then put the money into PR and expect results.

If your story is interesting, unique, and you come into the cannabis industry with good intentions, most of the time media influencers will be interested in you. Depending on the PR firm you work with, you'll likely pay a monthly deductible to keep them on board and unlock earned media placements and new partnerships that you wouldn't otherwise have thought of. This often makes public relations even more cost-effective than traditional pay-to-play marketing and advertising.

2. Build your brand image

It's just as important to actively tell your brand's story as it is to develop it in the beginning. From personal experience, salespeople yawn (often driven by numbers and the achievement of quantitative goals) when the branding conversation comes up, but here's the punch line: Stories sell. For a brand looking to develop a sustainable, long-term plan for themselves, creating, nurturing and telling a story that resonates with audiences is critical. Strategic public relations only reinforces the extent to which your story is being told.

Now more than ever it is of the utmost importance to get rid of the scars of cannabis branding, "urge Shane Hammer and Tyler Aldridge, founders of Design Kush." Thoughtful PR that is strategically set up with measurable measures can lay the groundwork to effectively shape perception and establish a world-class cannabis brand. PR campaigns can both increase engagement in the short term and improve SEO rankings in the long term, especially when combined with best practices for websites and other digital marketing strategies. "

3. Establish credibility

Can you blame consumers for trying to tell the great from the mean from the bad when hundreds of brands on the market claim they are the best option? As a collective, the cannabis industry has been better at educating consumers over the past eight to 12 months, but the majority of those new to cannabis still struggle to understand things like how the end cannabinoid system works, and which ones Products suit you?

The same applies to ancillary services in the B2B area. In an emerging industry, how do owners and operators know who to trust when they bring in an outside partner to grow their business and increase sales? Public relations that result in well-deserved media coverage in publications, podcasts, news outlets and magazines that people have already found believable to themselves will help cannabis leaders break out of the white noise of the industry and establish credibility as figures of authority within the space.

"To convey the balanced purpose of the company and to express the transition narrative in a light that can guide the uninformed, a balanced public relations firm can do for you," said Olanzo Jarrett, founder of DawaLife Inc. and Harmony Treats. "PR is an investment that helps keep your company relevant."

4. Build trust

Cannabis is still a burgeoning industry, making it hard for people to know who's coming to the table with good intentions and not just here to make money quickly. If you actively tell your story and do so in a way that positively attracts the attention of the local, regional, and national media, you will find that your target market grows bigger over time. The power of public relations in this regard is very similar to that of positive word of mouth.

5. Attract more of the right talent

Another by-product of strategic public relations is that you attract more of the right talent. If you're reading this, chances are you are in a position where you need to work on a team. For those of us who work in a team, we know how important it is not only to have qualified and talented employees by our side, but also to work with the right employees who recognize the culture of the company and see through everything the way to manifest it successfully.

REASONS PUBLIC RELATIONS MATTERS TO THE CANNABIS BUSINESS

Helps manage reputation

Public relations help manage reputation. Trusted media connections are a prerequisite for reputation management. For example, on your cannabis business journey, you will be faced with dire situations such as bad advertising or dissatisfied customers criticizing how bad your product is on social media. At times like these, media connections can help you repair the damage. Public Relations agencies give cannabis companies the opportunity to make such connections.

Promote brand values

In the cannabis industry, trust plays a critical role in determining whether or not the business will be successful. Lack of confidence can also lead to lost sales. However, when they hire someone in public relations, those experts can work and build credibility by enhancing an organization's reputation through pieces of thought leadership, influencer connections, and networking strategies. With the help of Public Relation, you can send positive messages to your audience that is in line with your brand image by using the ideas that your target customers respond to most positively.

Strengthen relationships with the cannabis community

Public relations strengthens the relationship with the cannabis community. When you make new connections, it means that you are building ties with the local market by joining groups, donating time to charities or any cause related to your business. Being an active member of a community establishes its trustworthiness. A good public relationship means building ongoing relationships with many important influencers and knowing how your cannabis business can become a great source of influence.

Public relations is opportunistic

Your public relations communications with influencers don't always have to be about your business. Offer accessibility to your consumers to help the influencer see how they solve problems with their cannabis products.

Public Relations Improves Your Cannabis Presence Online

In this world where everyone is digitally connected, Public Relation helps the cannabis industry make the most of its online presence. Not only can Public Relations agencies provide today's cannabis business with the support and guidance they need to market themselves online, but these companies may also be ready to step in when disaster strikes or something goes wrong with the reputation that it has been. trying to build. With the help of social media, press releases, and connections to promotional sites that post content, PR companies can help the cannabis industry achieve its desired things and overcome obstacles that could prevent them from succeeding. Through its Public Relations activity, the company monitors the interests of cannabis consumers, partners and employees, identifies threats, helps the industry resolve various conflicts, and quickly establishes a dialogue.

CHAPTER 22

BUSINESS BANKRUPTCY AND

RECEIVERSHIP

Business bankruptcy

Business bankruptcy is when a business owner goes to federal court for assistance in eliminating and repaying debt with the protection and guidance of a bankruptcy court. Through the bankruptcy process and under careful observation by federal courts, individuals and companies can restructure their financial situation at the discretion of the bankruptcy courts without creditors' interference.

All types of bankruptcy are governed by Title 11 of the United States Code.

The aim of bankruptcy is to reorganize the debtor - in our case the company that is indebted to its sellers and / or investors - with the aim of "starting over" at the end of the process and getting better business prospects and fairness to creditors, all related to contractual priorities. The economic efficiency of bankruptcy relies on the fact that the management of the organization can remain intact (at least for a period of time) and the process is aimed at maintaining and maximizing the going concern value of the company.

There are several types of federal bankruptcies that are most common for businesses:

Chapter 7: business bankruptcy, or liquidation. In this scenario, the debts of the business are so substantial that it is not economically feasible to restructure them. The business is usually dissolved.

Chapter 13: personal bankruptcy (sole proprietors are eligible to file for Chapter 13). In this scenario, the individual files a repayment plan with the bankruptcy court.

Chapter 11: is generally the first choice for debtors without better out-of-court options. They provide immediate recourse to creditors' remedial action ("automatic stay") and allow further business financing through the use of "cash collateral" or whatever called "debtor in possession financing". It generally allows management to continue doing business, albeit with restrictions, and sets rules and deadlines for restructuring negotiations. It also provides a framework for balance sheet restructuring, as well as tools for operational restructuring, including the rejection of certain onerous contracts (e.g., employment contracts, leases, and delivery commitments). The ultimate goal of Chapter 11 is to preserve the value of the company through a restructuring plan that is subject to the approval of creditors, although the restructuring could later turn into liquidation.

Insolvency proceedings can be initiated through voluntary registration (in which the insolvent debtor has immediate bankruptcy protection) or through involuntary registration (initiated by bodies other than the debtor). As you can probably imagine, some of the most common warning signs of bankruptcy filing are:

- ➢ Covenant Default (s) and / or poor financial results
- ➢ Late / poor financial reporting
- ➢ Lack of cash / payment default
- ➢ Retention of financial / restructuring advisors by the debtor
- ➢ Significant company or industry-oriented developments
- ➢ Material litigation or legal or regulatory changes
- ➢ New displacement technologies or products

The preparation of the filing requires experts (usually lawyers and specialist advisors) to assist with the filing and filing of documents. The process involves the participation of a U.S. trustee as well as all secured and unsecured creditor parties. This process can be costly and time consuming. If the bankruptcy option were available to the entire cannabis industry, another implication would be that the court has no industry experience and the participating parties may not be sufficiently organized to succeed in what they seek to achieve through the trial.

Receivership

Receivership is a financial process in which a trustee (a legally appointed custodian) restructures the business to avoid bankruptcy. Receivership allows a court-appointed person to seek to reverse the business or assist with the liquidation of assets and the payment of obligations, including debts, to investors.

Receivership is a great option for cannabis investors if the company has incurred debt or has been offered an interest in the company. With an equity agreement, the company has no obligation to reimburse you. As a result, you can leave your cannabis store reception agreement empty-handed. However, if you are in a debt relationship, bankruptcy administration can help you regain some financial resources from the cannabis business. This is also a great option if you have a joint venture with a cannabis company and you owe money outside of the business. This is considered a debt that must be repaid. Marijuana receptions have many unique properties and are not for the inexperienced court recipient. It does not matter how many reception points you have managed. Unless you have specifically managed a reception point for marijuana dishes, chances are you are not familiar with the challenges you may face. The purpose of this information is to help you determine what assistance, if any, you may need if you are called through a marijuana trial.

Receivership is a great option for those looking to exit the cannabis market and still want to recoup some of the resources they invested in this business. The Receivership has a nuance that makes it an attractive option for investors. If you have a debt guarantee or loan for a cannabis business, you can ask a court to receive that cannabis business. The company has no choice but to be taken over by a court-appointed recipient and out of the hands of the current operator.

WHAT ROLE DOES A COURT-APPOINTED RECEIVERSHIP PLAY?

A receiver's job is to oversee the recovery or closure of the business. This can include liquidating real estate, paying off creditors, and delivering the remaining value to shareholders. All management decisions are made by the recipient; Any authority of the directors or owners of the organization is delegated to the recipient by court order. The court may also allow the recipient to borrow funds to keep the organization running while it attempts to resolve ongoing claims. A recipient can participate in legal proceedings "for or against" the company. The recipient can sell any assets in the organization and settle claims on behalf of the organization.

Neutrality is decisive for the role of the receiver. "A recipient must not have a relationship with any of the parties or a court or have an interest in the company. Additionally, the recipient must avoid all potential conflicts of interest and disclose any potential conflicts at the time of the appointment, "writes one expert. There can be no conflict of interest for any recipient, company or otherwise. A recipient is prohibited from profiting financially from her position or using her position for the benefit of family members, business partners and other social relationships.

WHAT POWERS DOES A RECEIVERSHIP HAVE?

The general job of a recipient is to conduct all business activities in a financially responsible manner. Specific benefits of a recipient include:

1. Assume the role and exercise the powers of all positions such as General Director and General Director. Manage the day-to-day operations of the company along with the reception process.

2. Borrow funds to cover ongoing administration costs and other cash flow needs.

3. Pay the amounts necessary to maintain, maintain, protect or improve the assets and property of the company.

4. Reimbursement and discharge of liens, claims or fees of any kind for the assets and property of the organization.

5. Investigate all legal claims made by and against the company and take appropriate legal action to respond to such claims.

6. Representation in all aspects of the company, its shareholders and creditors.

7. Hire other professionals such as lawyers, accountants, and tax advisers to assist you throughout the reception process. If necessary, hire other staff to manage the organization during the reception.

8. Sell a mortgage, deed of trust, stocks, debt, or property (tangible and intangible) for cash.

9. "Buy or lease offices, automobiles, furniture, equipment and supplies, and contract the insurance, professional and technical services necessary to carry out the reception."

10. Resolve claims against or in favor of the company; Dispose of any asset or property that is classified as "incriminating."

11. Use the organization's assets to pay all reception costs.

CONCLUSION

Finally, cannabis use has spread among adolescents and adolescents in many developed and other developing countries. In developing countries with a long history of use, a large number of consumers continue to use it centrally and abroad. There are several side effects of cannabis use. Using cannabis destroys work during operation and using it prior to transportation can increase the risk of injury.

Marijuana needs to be legalized as tax dollars would bring in millions of dollars for our government and help us generate money that could be used for useful purposes like schools and public health. Cannabis-related crime is falling as a significant source of funding comes from violent groups and international organizations. Law enforcement agencies can focus on violent crime and not waste the resources of cannabis users. Recognition of the law will give space in our prisons and open to criminals who need to be there. People who do not practice traditional medicine feel comfortable and do not have to worry about pain and discomfort. Adults have the opportunity to enjoy drugs that do not cause serious side effects. Eventually,

Taxation will know how much money is being spent on medical cannabis, and we believe marijuana will be accepted across the United States. Cannabis does not prevent something from being used to stop its use. Time to stop fighting cannabis.

CPSIA information can be obtained
at www.ICGtesting.com
Printed in the USA
BVHW070415161221
624023BV00012B/1161